Bus 9 to
Paradise

Also by Leo Buscaglia

Love

Because I Am Human

The Way of the Bull

The Disabled and Their Parents:
A Counseling Challenge

Personhood

The Fall of the Freddie the Leaf

Living, Loving & Learning

Loving Each Other

Leo Buscaglia

Bus 9 to Paradise

A Loving Voyage

Edited by
Daniel Kimber

Fawcett Columbine • New York

In Memory of
David Hall

Table
of
Contents

PROLOGUE

I was in Melbourne, Australia, with my publisher promoting a new book. Such tours are usually very demanding and this was no exception. So, when we were finally granted a day of rest, we agreed to spend it out-of-doors, away from hotels, bookstores, T.V. studios and radio stations. The warm, clear day seemed perfect for a walk through one of Melbourne's quaint suburbs. Our goal was the city zoo.

On our way we stopped at a bus stop, hoping that it might offer us some indication that we were going in the right direction. The schedule, mounted on a tall pole, clearly listed times of bus arrivals and departures. We were suddenly struck with a designation that read, "Bus 9 to Paradise." How beautiful it sounded . . . Bus 9 to Paradise. We thought, "Wouldn't it be nice if we could actually ride on a bus destined for Paradise?" We wondered what it would be like; whether after we got there, would it be truly our idea of heaven.

In Dante's classic, *The Divine Comedy*, he pictured paradise as a vision of the rose, his metaphor for the purest kind of love. Mark Twain, on the other hand, created a much more down-to-earth, life-on-the-Mississippi scene. The Argentine author, Jorge Luis Borges, always imagined paradise "as a kind of library."

I'm sure each of us dreams of a paradise with visions no less idyllic than the poets, philosophers and artists. For some, paradise conjures dreams of limitless green pastures and refreshing waters reflecting skies of rainbows. For others, it is a gold-red dusk over the Manhattan skyline. Some of us envision a land free of anxiety and pressures, with soothing tones of celestial angel choruses. Others would opt for fresh challenges accompanied by New Orleans jazz bands or the abandoned, joyous growl of a B.B. King. Some would wish for tranquility and peaceful silence.

It's obvious that if there were to be an actual earthly paradise, it would be a very personal creation. There would certainly be no easy transport, no designated "Bus 9." This undiscovered territory has no common destination. (Isn't it interesting and wonderful that we don't even agree about paradise?)

We did not take Bus 9 to Paradise. I'm happy that we didn't for it seems clear that paradise is to be found only in our own immense and limitless minds, shaped by our own unique experience and willingness to continually grow and change. If there is a commonality, it seems to me to be that *life is paradise for those who love many things with a passion:* people, food, flowers, music, dance, books, art, memories, poetry, family, learning—an endless list. There is no need to seek paradise in some far-off future. The more passionately we love many things, the closer we come to living our paradise NOW.

Bus 9 to Paradise

*LIFE IS
PARADISE
FOR THOSE
WHO
LOVE
MANY
THINGS
WITH A
PASSION!*

A
Passion
for
Loving

Perhaps it's time to look again at the ways and power of love. For many, just the thought that love is a real possibility gives hope to what could otherwise be an empty life. What harm can come from mutual respect, gentleness, goodness, trust and peaceful coexistence? Think about it. Only love has the power to unite without taking away another's dignity, another's self. Only love holds no jealous possession over people and nations. Only love is capable of putting humanity before ideology or race. Only love can supply the endless energies required to overcome hunger and despair.

"Love one another." These words were spoken more than two thousand years ago. Powerful though this command is, many of us have succeeded in ignoring it for these many years. We all give lip service to it but few of us expect anyone to really practice it. We leave that to madmen and saints.

In fact, we have become suspicious of lovers and either dismiss them as naive and irrelevant, or we see them as phonies. We are certain that no one could really care about anyone else without having some ulterior motive. The qualities of love such as tenderness, commitment, concern, generosity and trust are relegated to the realm of platitudes and are ignored.

Today the phrase "love one another" takes on a more urgent tone. It seems to me that we must love one another or die. Modern society shrugs off still another plea for love. It is amused by the suggestion that the world could be cemented together, not by the threat of holocaust or an arms race, but through a deep respect for life. No one will deny that we have reached a critical point in our history. In fact, there are growing numbers of fatalists who believe we have reached a point of no return. One thing is painfully obvious. Conventional methods to bring peace and understanding to our world have failed.

The more we look about us, the more we find hate, violence, prejudice and disregard for human life. We listen to newscasters and read columnists who deal out statistics about war dead, starvation, children being abused and sacrificed, disregard for human dignity and human rights. And all with about as much feeling as a report of the day's football scores. We are becoming conditioned to a whole spectrum of wasted human potential. Still, we continue to ignore love as a possible alternative.

I recall the shock I felt when I was traveling in the Soviet Union and a man I met in Odessa said to me, "Why do you want to kill us?" I tried to make him understand that I wanted to kill no one, that I celebrated life, not death. Somewhere buried in our respective ideologies were two people trying to relate their very real and very human concerns—not only for the world, but for each other as individuals. Through the magic of caring communication, we accomplished a victory of sorts—we forgot about all the things that separated us and were soon lost in one another. At that instant all contradictions and symbols were refuted. We both chose life.

I am sure that many would respond to this as naive and unrealistic; that love is barely strong enough to maintain most close family relationships and that beyond that, the heart is strained to its limits. So it is ridiculous for anyone to count on the power of love for a solution to international problems. I've often been told that in my zeal to love everyone I risk ending up loving no one. Nothing can be farther from the truth. Universal love is not only possible, it is the most complete love of which we are capable as human beings.

But love can only work when we give up the antiquated mindsets which continue to paralyze us. We need to challenge the sophisticates who view it as romantic nonsense, idealistic bosh, unscientific and anti-intellectual. We need to accept love in our life as the most universal force for unification and good, accessible to all who really want it.

Only then will we discover that love, fully realized, has the power to lay aside the petty things which separate us and reveal the fact that our *enemy* has a face and a heart. It is at this point that all things again become possible.

There are those who are certain they can solve all the issues and problems of the day with one solution. Regardless of the topic of discussion, they invariably return to their theories as being at the heart of the matter. I have been accused of being preoccupied with the topic of love and wanting to apply it to all life situations. Since I've been doing this for over thirty years, I am often mistakenly labeled an authority on the subject. The expectation is that I can offer guidance or solutions in all matters relating to love.

If someone were to claim to be an authority on life we would quite properly dismiss them as ridiculous. Life encompasses us, not the other way around. The topic of love in all its manifestations is also all encompassing. I have found that it invites us more to share in experiences than to strive to be exalted teachers. So when I suggest that we learn to love more each day, it's a tired cliché only if we regard the words of the message instead of the powerful challenge it presents.

I believe that we are all searching for something that will make existence more meaningful. We want to get outside of ourselves and mingle our lives with others. We hope to become better lovers and more complete human beings. Sometimes we can learn from the examples of others. My purpose as a teacher is to facilitate growth. If in sharing the thoughtful phrases of an ancient philosopher or in suggesting that we strive for a greater vision of the future, the purpose is sound, I consider it a labor of love to continue my work.

So I ask you again to consider the tremendous power of love, not simply as an abstraction, but as a dynamic, tangible force. It is an energy source that is never diminished by its use; it gives us the strength and security to challenge ourselves and others to change and grow.

And there is also a quieter power of love we often fail to recognize. Babe Ruth, immortalized for his prowess with a baseball bat, revealed this less-noted strength when he talked about the famous people in his life who never signed an autograph, but who wrote their names on just a few simple hearts. If each of us were to recollect our sharpest, most vivid memories, I would be willing to bet that the moments of love and the people who were part of them are the most permanently etched.

Many of us still act as if we believe that the real wonder of love lies in the magical effect it has in making people lose their appetite, get weak in the knees and generally succumb to a sort of general anesthesia.

When we learn to expand our definition of love, we find that many other incredible things are possible. A single phone call out of the blue to tell people we're thinking about them can set the mood of an entire day on both ends of the line. A single compliment can accomplish the same thing. We will move mountains for people who make us feel special by their love and caring.

Admittedly, this is not the stuff of torrid romance novels. They are, however, meaningful examples of the power of love. They remind us that words such as hopeless and impossible have no meaning in the context of loving one another.

There is also a transcendent power of love, one that was working before we were born and that guaranteed us a whole army of people who would love us no matter what. And ultimately, there is the faith which, in all religions, tells us of another kind of love which lasts beyond any concept of time.

I think we'd all agree that to go through life without a true friend is to have missed one of the most satisfying and challenging of human experiences. Still, each day people live and die among strangers, alone, never having experienced a real friend.

We humans have an instinctual need to be close to one another. We have people around us almost continually—people we know casually, see occasionally or meet in brief daily encounters. Some of them we call friends, but what we actually mean is acquaintances. To have a friend means something very different—more of a sacred thing. Aristotle described friendship as "one soul in two bodies."

Friendship involves two people committed to each other over a long period of time—through conflict, joy, unhappiness and change. Most of us take our friendships for granted. We become passive in maintaining them and lose sight of the fact that they need constant effort, care and attention.

Emerson, in his stunning essay, *Of Friendship*, said, "We take care of our health, we make our roof tight and clothing sufficient, but who provides wisely that we should not be wanting in the best property of all—friends?" He adds, "The best way to have a friend is to be one." Most of us have found this to be true. We take such care and guard so closely the things we treasure, but are so often lax with the special gift of friendship. If we really gave some thought to it, we would work harder to keep these special bonds growing and strong. There are few things in life which offer us greater rewards.

A short time ago I lost a special friend to death. Both of us had valued and nurtured our relationship for over twenty-five years. During that period we were often separated by time or circumstance, but we were determined never to allow anything to interfere with our ever-growing friendship. I've often thought of our varied experiences, of the changes each of us went through and of the bonds which made us friends for life.

My friend helped me to see myself in all my human

imperfections while he revealed his own. Together, we gave each other room to make mistakes, the strength to meet frustration and even failure, because we knew that we would always have the other to fall back on, to offer support and encouragement to start over.

We hurt or disappointed each other from time to time, but from this we learned to practice the delicate art of human forgiveness until we reached the point when we could look beyond the hurt rather than backward in anger and resentment. We stopped judging and censuring. We each knew that when the other was foolish or had lapses, it was never a permanent condition.

We shared our most personal thoughts, feelings, ideas, plans and dreams. When there was a conflict to be resolved, we discovered the real mutual benefits of friendship which we could have found in no other way. We became mirrors to one another, each reflecting the other's uniqueness from a different perspective. We were often required to test our friendship, having to see how much we would be willing to do and give to keep it alive over the years. It's an overworked adage, but nonetheless true, that you can always tell who your true friends are when you are in need.

To lose my dear friend after so many years of loving investment was terribly painful. It was difficult to part with such a positive force in my life. But nothing is forever. In reality we never lose the people we love. They become immortal through us. They continue to live in our hearts and minds. They participate in our every act, idea and decision. No one will ever replace them and in spite of the pain we are richer for all the years invested in them. Because of them, we have so much more to bring to our present relationships and all those to come.

•   •   •

I recently sat with a despondent friend whose husband had sought what he thought were greener fields and found them. He left my friend and their two children with the casualness of one taking off on a holiday cruise. Echoing a recently read self-help book, he said he had a right to happiness and his greatest responsibility was to himself. He was hoping that he could still have a friendship with his wife and, of course, unlimited visiting privileges with his children.

His wife had other ideas. She was bitter, hurt and vindictive. He had shattered her ego and broken up the family. In no way was she about to maintain a friendship with him. In fact she was quick to call him a rodent and several expletives I had never heard her use before!

She turned to me, a friend, for help. She couldn't seem to stop crying. She'd lost interest in her home and her children. Though she continued to work, she found that always being so upset and distracted caused her to be negative in her interactions with others. She snapped at friends, became impatient with coworkers in the office and found herself shouting at the children.

She continued to find endless reasons for hating her ex-husband, but she also began to hate herself in the process. She was filled with regrets and self-recriminations. She was certain that if she had done more for him—made herself more attractive, kept a better home—she wouldn't have lost him and the children would still have a father.

How could I help her? No amount of tears or regrets were going to bring her husband back or revitalize the dead marriage. I am never one to offer advice. I gave that up years ago. I'm as confused as everyone else. How can I tell others what to do? Anyway, there was no easy solution. Damaged egos require long healing periods.

She could not continue in her present state. Prolonged despair was already taking its toll. Of course, there were many things she could do. Among them, it seemed to me, she could finally face that fact that life does go on. She was still young, attractive and capable, and just because her husband had obviously devalued these traits, he was really just one person of many. It was not a matter of comparing herself with the other woman. There was no basis for comparison. Armed with this reality, I suggested that she might accept the situation, forgive her husband for his actions and herself for whatever part she might have unconsciously played in his decision.

We discussed that much of her pain was based on the fact that she was taking responsibility for her husband's acts. I reminded her that since she was the innocent victim it seemed unrealistic for her to take on so much guilt, so many tears. She became irate! "Forgive him!" she said, horrified. "Are you crazy? I'd die first! I'll find a way someday to get even with him. I'll find a way to hurt him like he hurt me!" Her face took on a frightening look. Fresh tears fell as she refused to let go of her anger.

Her husband was off celebrating a new life with new possibilities and a new person, none of which she had any control over. She, on the other hand, was drowning in despair. Most of us have learned from experience that not to forgive hurts *us* more than anyone else. Why do we find it so hard to forgive?

Grudges carried for a lifetime are a pretty heavy load. In addition to adding wrinkles to brows, they create much bitterness and suspicion. No one is guiltless. If we hope to be forgiven for our actions or shortcomings, we might start by attempting to forgive others for theirs. There is not always justice. Sometimes we have to forgive even when we've been wronged, for our own sake.

Perhaps my friend will one day realize that she did the best she could in their relationship at the time, and that her husband thought he had done the same. Certainly I am not condoning his actions, but in the act of forgiving we release ourselves from bondage. It then becomes possible for us to move forward and love again, wiser for the experience.

A man once told me that his dog's love was the only love in his life of which he was sure. He explained, "He always greets me with enthusiasm, he is responsive to my touch, he's forgiving, and he's there when I need him. He loves me without conditions." This was quite a statement! Either the people in this man's life had fallen short of giving him the assurance he needed, or his idea of love needed redefining.

In human relationships we are seldom guaranteed such unequivocal love and we are often given to wonder whether we are in fact loved by those closest to us. Since our definitions of love are constantly changing as we learn more about giving it each day, it's not unusual that we question whether or not we are receiving it.

A wife says to a husband (or vice versa),

"Do you love me?"

"Of course," he replies.

"Why?" she presses for a more definitive answer.

"What do you mean why? I've been married to you for twenty years, haven't I?"

How satisfied would we be if we presented someone with a vintage wine and upon asking his opinion of it he replied, "I'm drinking it, aren't I?"

Love, as intangible, as complex, and as personal as it is, still needs expression between those who share it. No two people express their love in the same way, and it is that unique expression which makes love the most powerful and enduring of life's forces.

Love is as encompassing as life itself, and when we seek to define it we sometimes end up imposing limits on it. We can, however, attempt to describe it, and in so doing, better understand it. One of the most beautiful descriptions I've ever read is from Corinthians I, and even as well known as it is, is still well worth repeating:

> Love is patient and kind; love is not jealous or conceited or proud; love is not ill mannered, or selfish, or irritable; love does not keep a record of wrongs: Love is not happy with evil but is happy with the truth. Love never gives up: its faith, hope, and patience never fail. Love is eternal . . . There are faith, hope and love, these three; but the greatest of these is love.

So, for the question, "How do I know when I am truly loved?" there can be only partial answers that need elaboration and the special touch that each of us brings to a relationship. Certainly, though, when we are loved, the people who love us want us to be what we are, not what they are. They rejoice in the fact that we are growing with our ideas, our dreams, our uniqueness, our future. They want us to be independent and free, not submissive and afraid. The people who love us want to simplify our existence, not be protecting us from pain, but by being there when we need them. They encourage risk because they understand that by risking we continue to grow. They help us to find alternatives for behavior, rejoicing in our success and comforting us in our failure. They are not only lovers, but friends, loyal and willing to make allowances for our imperfections. They can be counted on for support and companionship.

Each of us has different requirements for how much and what kind of love we receive. Some of us need to hear the words, "I love you," each day, while for others, the words are contained in a look, an attitude, an unspoken communication. No matter how love is expressed, the important thing is that it be communicated freely and often.

I receive letters from a variety of people who all have a similar tale to tell: the love seems to have gone out of their relationship. "He's not nearly as romantic as he was when we first dated." "She's not the same girl I fell in love with."

I prefer to think of love as something we *grow* into, not something we fall in and out of. I also believe that it is something that cannot be limited by one person's definition or demands of what it should be. There are always at least two sides to any love relationship.

An expression of love is the most basic of human assurances. When it is given freely and without condition, it can only strengthen and give greater purpose to a relationship.

Any number of psychology textbooks will tell us that our basic patterns of behavior are most influenced in our early years by our parents. Mom and Dad are credited (but more often it seems, faulted) for their part as role models. Some people live their lives believing that their inability to express love as they would like to stems from the fact that their parents didn't teach them to love. And so they state that the die is cast and the past becomes a convenient scapegoat to explain or rationalize their chronic loneliness and lovelessness.

We should never subscribe to any idea that even suggests that human behavior, whatever its origin, cannot be changed. There is great hope for those of us who feel that we lack the ability to love fully and joyfully without fear. That hope lies in the knowledge that we can dedicate ourselves to the process of learning to love *today*. As we attempt to live in love, we'll understand that pain, discomfort, and even rejection are very much a part of the process. Loving will require courage, resiliency and hope, and will never come to people who give up easily. But since love is the most rewarding of human experiences, it is certainly worth the risk.

A student who attended my Love Class some years ago was inspired by one of our discussions and decided to go directly home and sweep his wife off her feet, bringing new love into their lives. Understandably, after ten years of marriage devoid of outward shows of affection, she became suspicious of his real motives.

"Why this sudden love offering after so many years?" she pondered. He had either gone crazy or he was feeling guilty about something. When she faced him with these suspicions he was thoroughly incensed over her reaction. He fully expected her to sing hallelujahs and fall into his arms. Instead he was received with doubt, suspicion, and rejection. And so, as often happens under such conditions, he retreated into the safety and habit of his unromantic self. Love had failed him. He even justified this by declaring that he had tried and that therefore it wasn't his fault. It was his wife who wasn't a lover.

This man may have been in earnest about wanting to become a more loving person, but he really wasn't prepared to encounter the complexity of feelings love can create. Nor was he willing to commit himself to the idea that learning to love does not happen overnight but requires time, effort, and patience.

Ours is a culture that offers "how to" information on every conceivable subject. Television programs, self-help books, manuals, articles, etc. are continually showing us the way to a better personality, a more beautiful body, more friends, or less fears. They tell us how to become sexual acrobats or just how to grow a better petunia. We think nothing of investing our time and money in developing a better backhand or having the greenest lawn on the block and yet we hold back at the least suggestion that the same effort might be necessary if we desire to become more loving individuals. This would be a better world if we would exert the same amount of zeal we apply to our hobbies to the infinitely more satisfying goal of becoming better lovers.

Most of us can remember the story of Ebenezer Scrooge and his amazing transformation from a hateful and heartless old man to a kind and loving one, all in one night. That this beloved story and others like it are told year after year for generations suggests the timeless value we hold for a life transformed by love. Most of us however, barring the visitation of a helpful ghost, will have to be the architects of our own change, and accept the fact that it may not happen overnight.

If we must begin at square one, then so be it. The important thing is that we begin now. Each new moment of love experienced and learned leads to more such moments, and moment to moment we make this a better world for ourselves and for all those we encounter.

I learned long ago how profoundly disappointing unfulfilled expectations can be. The lesson has stayed with me. It happened one Christmas when I was in my teens. I remember the sudden appearance under my family's Christmas tree of the largest present I had ever hoped to see. It stood at least a foot taller than I and was twice as heavy; and, wonder of wonders, it had my name on it. For two whole weeks before Christmas, this present towered above all others, and it defied any conventional attempts to learn of its contents before its time.

Those two weeks seemed an eternity. I could think of little else. My mind was filled with imaginings. Because of its size and mystery, that gift created an aura of sheer magic for me.

When the day of days arrived, my family gathered in celebration. The main attraction was to be the opening of my present. How many times in the past two weeks I had anticipated this moment. Even as I was opening it, I remember experiencing a vague sense of disappointment— the Great Mystery was about to end and I would no longer be able to engage in my soaring dreams.

It was a handmade desk that my Uncle Louie had painstakingly built. It was certainly beautiful and much needed. But by this time nothing of this world could have satisfied my expectations. I can't imagine what I had expected. Still, in that disappointment was a lesson that would last a lifetime.

Buddha once wrote that, "When we cease expecting, we have all things." If we expect nothing, we are always delighted. When we have expectations, no matter how much we get, we tend to expect more. We can hope that everyone will love us, but we cannot expect them to. In realizing this, we free ouselves and others of the burden of conforming to our expectations. When others say, "you must love me, I'm your wife, husband, mother, brother, lover, etc.," they forget that love can only be given freely. And no matter how much we demand it, it will come only when it is freely offered.

Most of us enter relationships with a set of expectations that have been steadily accumulating and waiting for just the right person to fill them. If the list is long and the demands are rigid, the wait can be a lifetime. The whole idea that we expect others to behave in a prescribed manner or conform to a preset image denies them their most precious asset, their uniqueness, and puts them into the category of a commodity.

What attracts us to others are usually the qualities that make them unique. Instead of rejoicing in their uniqueness, we attempt to fit them into neat little categories and expect them to perform accordingly. How much better it would be to bury expectations and relate to the individual we love—as the remarkable, singularly unique person that he or she is. A person who will never come this way again.

Teachers must constantly avoid preconceived notions of their students for the simple reason that they become self-fulfilling prophecies. Students who are expected to perform a certain way because of their race, appearance, family, or background, invariably play the role in which they are cast and consequently are prevented from being themselves.

A friend of mine once told me that he was continually disenchanted with his dates. In each instance on a first date, he was certain he would meet the love of his life. Of course, no girl could meet his requirements as wife, mother, housekeeper, entertainer, sex symbol, and conversationalist. It took him years of disappointment before he discovered that it was actually more fun (and certainly more realistic) to discover each girl as an individual, and allow her to reveal herself as she was, not as he dreamed her. He was soon happily married.

To avoid the inevitable disappointment of unfulfilled expectations, we should expect only of ourselves. In this way we will free others to be themselves while we stretch and grow to our fullest potential.

A Passion for Joy

The pursuit of happiness is perhaps our most basic drive. It is even mentioned in our Declaration of Independence. How we pursue it, and even how we define it, varies from person to person. Perhaps what makes it so elusive is our problem in not only not knowing how to obtain it, but how to keep it around. Our highest spirits can be so quickly conquered by adversity.

The well-known writer William S. Burroughs recently stated in an interview that for him, happiness is a by-product of "function, purpose and conflict; that those who seek happiness for itself seek victory without war."

Ancient Egyptians believed that upon their death they would be asked by the god Osiris two questions and their answers would determine whether they could continue their journey in the afterlife. The first question was, "Did you bring joy?" The second was, "Did you find joy?" These goals then become a sacred charge in life and the only way to obtain eternal happiness.

These are questions no less vital today than they were in ancient Egypt. They are ones we must continually ask ourselves. Most of us have our own strong sense of purpose to celebrate life and spread all the joy we can.

Think of the happiest people you know. They're the ones who seem to be able to find joy everywhere. If we study these people very closely and analyze just how they do it, we may find some answers far simpler than we would have believed. We've heard them before:

"There's good in every person. It's up to me to bring it out."

"There is a light side of everything if you look for it."

"I see each new day as a challenge. What I make of it is up to me."

Our search for happiness and our capacity to bring it to others leads us back to ourselves, for we start by finding joy in ourselves. The inner joy we develop becomes the wellspring from which we draw to use in every encounter.

I am amazed at the human capacity to find joy even in the harshest extremes, the cruelest of fates, the stories of people with broken bodies but whose spirits remain high. We admire their courage but seldom consider the profound example they provide for all of us, especially those of us who hide behind despair and hopelessness.

As a teacher, I used to encourage my students to keep a journal as a record of their innermost thoughts and feelings. Occasionally I would ask that they show them to me for our discussion. I noticed a tendency in them to emphasize the negative in life. There were the "Oh, woe is me," stories. The "Life is miserable, boring, depressing, confusing, unfair, cruel, etc., etc." stories. Each day seemed to be a test of endurance rather than an adventure.

"Why don't you write of the joy in your life?" I would ask them. "It's really your choice."

The answer was always that the bad things just seemed to have more impact than the good things. They seemed to take joy for granted. Their problems touched them more deeply than their moments of joy. That notion is perhaps what inspired a study done a few years ago to determine the dominant mood of currently popular songs. The findings revealed that about three-fourths of the songs dealt with the pain and anguish of love. You know the type:

"You broke my heart, I'm so alone,
All day long, I sit and moan."

Or a current favorite, "Love is a Battlefield." (Whatever happened to "Love is a Many-Splendored Thing"?)

Soap operas so frequently capture this spirit with their unending tales of sorrow and affliction. People say that their soaps help them endure their own problems. But we need more out of life than just physical ease and freedom from care. Our goldfish have that.

The happiness in life that we all seek so often involves what we give to others. Ancient Egyptians understood that finding joy in life and bringing it to others were one and the same. It is as Louis Mann once wrote, that "Happiness is a perfume which you cannot pour on others without getting a few drops on yourself."

Isn't it strange how suspicious we sometimes are of happiness? If we have it we are somehow sure that it can't last. We're certain that misery can't be too far off. We have a vague feeling that we'll be punished for prolonged joy.

The great author of madness, Luigi Pirandello, tells a story of a man who was so frightened by joy that it drove him mad. When he found the woman of his dreams he was so certain he'd lose her that he feigned disinterest until he almost did lose her. When he planned their honeymoon his anxiety reached the breaking point. He told everyone that they would be going to Florence and Venice. Instead he took his bride to Naples—the opposite direction. He felt he could in this way trick the misery which would be trying to find him in Florence and Venice and would not know that he was having an ecstatic honeymoon in Naples!

Most of us are not quite that pathological, but perhaps we may recognize the symptoms. We feel that there is something not quite acceptable about having things go right for us. We begin to imagine despair around every corner until we bring it upon ourselves. I have a dear friend who, when everything in her life is fine, is sure that the next telephone call will be a message of personal catastrophe, every letter will be from the IRS or someone suing her, every telegram an announcement of the death of a loved one. Experience should have convinced her by this time that her fears are not reasonable, but she's always the same. Now she has added another problem. She's worried about her worrying!

When we were children we took for granted that each day would bring us greater happiness. We celebrated everything: flowers, animals, other children, loving adults, learning—we embraced them all with open arms and growing joy. I wonder what causes this joy to give way to cynicism later in life?

Some people are really bothered by others' happiness. They may even show real contempt for other people's joy, which they call naiveté. These are the people H.L.

Mencken once described. He said that they are so pessimistic that when they smell flowers, they immediately look for a coffin. This cynical attitude is usually brought on by envy. Being a little short on happiness makes some people want to believe that it's a universal condition.

There is a great deal of compassion for the miserable and we are eager to help make their lives better. But few of us see any need to help those who are already happy to remain so. We need them and should honor them.

William Phelps was right on target when he said, "If happiness consisted of physical ease and freedom from care, then the happiest individual would not be either a man or a woman, it would be an American cow!" We make our own happiness and it takes work. If we are living a happy life and have worked at making it so, we deserve it and have no reason to feel guilty about it.

There are days when I feel so good only my rational mind keeps me from levitating. People often accuse me of putting it on. They're certain that no one could feel *that* good. They know that I have the same problems they do. My health leaves a little to be desired. I have all sorts of demands made on me. They wonder what I have to be so happy about. My response is simple: I'm still alive and there is still so much more to do, to experience, to love. Why shouldn't I be happy?

Perhaps we object so much to another's happiness because it may prove to us that living happily in our crazy, mixed-up world is possible. We'd rather think that it isn't. It gives us an excuse not to work at it. We can say that happy people are living an illusion, that they are ignorant and unaware, that they can't be in touch with reality. All this, in spite of the fact that we can know happiness if we learn to embrace it.

The despair which we believe to be lurking around each dark corner mostly exists in our minds. Everyone en-

counters it but only some of us honor it. It's possible that
we will know even more happiness around that same corner. Perhaps it's true that happiness begets more happiness. I know there are some who are reading this and
thinking, "That Buscaglia is more naive than I thought."
Perhaps so, but as we are all traveling to the same destination, at least I can say I'm making the journey with joy
in my heart and a smile on my face. How about you?

One of the major problems in the world today is that
we've lost our sense of humor—this seems especially true
of our leaders. An intriguing fantasy for me would be a
great conference of the world's nations where, instead of
politicians or statesmen, each country would send its leading humorists to represent it. Instead of an aura of pomp
and seriousness that would normally be dictated by such
an occasion, there would prevail a lightheartedness, with
an assembly of individuals bent on raising spirits instead
of suspicions.

Behind it all would be the assumption that very few
things in this world so instantly form a common bond
among people as laughter. It's a universal language that
requires no interpretation. Serious problems needn't be ad-
dressed only by serious-minded people.

I place this idea in the realm of fantasy because I understand all too well the time-honored convention of sober
thought and strict decorum that exists whenever political
leaders come together to iron out their differences. This is
true even though we know that in interpersonal relationships, nothing can defuse a problem more readily than a
good laugh. Perhaps it is my own naiveté that leads me to
believe that diplomats could be guided by the same
principle.

I'm sure our humorists and comedians will never be elevated to the status of diplomats, but I shall always maintain that they are among our most beneficial physicians. Anyone who makes us laugh and convinces us not to take ourselves too seriously is contributing directly to our physical and mental well-being. As the most recent medical research tells us, laughter can be the best medicine. I often wonder how many modern-day neuroses are based, at least in part, on people who have lost touch with the fact that life is a wondrous joke with all of us as the gag line.

A sense of humor helps us to forget, if even for a moment, our often inflated sense of seriousness and propriety. It is a declaration of our superiority over the woes and calamities that may befall us. I know a family that serves as a beautiful example of this. From the grandparents down to the youngest members, laughter is always present when they gather together, even in the face of gloom. One of the favorite stories they tell is about the morning of the great California earthquake in 1971. After the rumbling had ceased and everyone had gone about the house tentatively surveying the damage, they joined a small congregation of neighbors in the street. One of the daughters suddenly gasped and pointed to part of the house which had crumbled, exposing the bathroom toilet. The youngest son began to laugh at this most preposterous sight and commented that this would certainly cut down on bathroom use. The laughter became contagious as the rest of the family joined in while their dumbfounded neighbors looked on. In the retelling of this story, it is the remark of an elder neighbor that still brings the loudest roars of laughter: "Laughter at such a time—they must be crazy!"

Granted there is nothing inherently funny about the destruction of property, but here was a family who rose above the despair of the moment; and even, as their neighbor suggested, by being just a little crazy at that instant, saved the day from despair. It's a fact that all of us are just a little crazy and we are better off if we get in touch with our madness from time to time. (If you think you're not crazy—you're probably crazier than most!) This family's remembrance of that day is not just in the joy of recalling an amusing story, but also in a sense of pride they all share in this personal triumph of the human spirit.

Many people persist in suppressing the spirit of joy in the unfortunate belief that life is strictly serious business. We often view silliness or childishness as regressions in behavior instead of realizing that each of us has a ridiculous side and that the child in us is one of our most prized possessions. We cultivate refinement and sophistication at the expense of spontaneity and fun. Polite tittering substitutes for unrestrained laughter. Joyous impulses are moderated or lost altogether in deference to common sense or good taste.

In each of us there is a reservoir of joyous freedom— madness, if you will. It's a natural and splendid balance to our more serious, socially proper side which allows us to suspend from time to time our rules of decorum. Why not rejoice a bit in our foolishness? In a world that knows no shortage of nonsense, we shouldn't hesitate to happily and playfully add our own touch of insanity. It's one of the best ways I know to survive.

Americans are often portrayed as being forever busy. Tradition has it that our reverence for the work ethic is second to none. According to this image, even our leisure moments are crammed with pressing duties and obligations; things are always unfinished or in need of our attention. We seem in perpetual motion.

As with all stereotypes, there are too many exceptions

to take it all that seriously. Besides, worse things have been said about people than that they work too hard. The implication, though, is that overworkers have forgotten how to relax. I do know just such a person, whom I shall call Tom. His friends call him a workaholic. His doctor advised him to take up a nice, slow-paced, leisurely hobby—anything to divert him, body and mind, from his frantic routine. It was decided that vegetable gardening would be just the thing for him.

So, with a little plot of land, a few tools and some overalls, Tom set about to cultivate a few crops and a more tranquil personality. His approach, however, was no different from anything else he ever tried: Get in there and give it all you've got—which is an admirable trait so long as it is not an all-consuming one. Well, Tom's garden was a study in horticulture. His friends and neighbors were impressed not only with the garden, but with his determination to find peace in it.

What they were unaware of was his growing obsession with garden pests which were descending on his little patch. Each evening after coming home from work, he would charge out to the back yard to do battle. Every little invader was wiped out with a vengeance. After all, if vegetable gardening was to be his hobby, there had certainly better be some tangible results to show for it. When he began to lose sleep thinking about the possibility of his tomatoes being ravaged, Tom decided that growing vegetables was not the key to his serenity. Last I heard, he was practicing meditation. I wish him luck.

It does seem paradoxical that one's leisure time could ever be a source of anxiety or stress, yet I wonder how many of us have truly learned to relax, or, as Walt Whitman wrote, ". . . to loaf and invite the soul," or to arrive at the point when we don't think of time, even when papers are stacking up on the desk, or deadlines are coming up. Of course, if we do all this, we run the risk of being called lazy.

I remember being stranded many years ago in a town just outside of Paris. It was toward midday and I needed a mechanic to put some life back into my rented Citroen. Of course, all shops were closed and all activity was at a standstill. It was merely the customary two-hour lunch time that was being observed. Think of it! Two hours for lunch. Time to eat, to take a nap, visit, or just disengage from the day's activity for a while. What was there to do? So I took a walk and found myself lying on a shaded hillside overlooking an old abandoned barn. I lay there trying to remember the last time I had done something like this.

When I awoke from an enchanting sleep, I felt a deep sense of calm. I walked slowly back from that hillside, thankful for the delay, and resolved not to run through the rest of my agenda without enjoying it.

One of the directions in which our technology seems to be leading us is more leisure time. Our work force is increasingly becoming mechanized and computerized, leaving us with the challenge of a whole new dimension in freedom. In meeting that challenge, I hope we may learn to seek out hidden paths of our potential. We may take the time to know ourselves and each other better, and come to understand our intimate connection with all living things. Perhaps we may also learn to have more control over our own destiny. We may learn that sometimes to do nothing is to do something.

Everyone loves to play. Playfulness is instinctive and it is universal. All forms of life play: dolphins, chimpanzees, squirrels, dogs, cats—all take time to play. They splash, chase, rough-and-tumble, tease and tickle. We love to watch their playfulness and stand for hours envying them their fun.

Was it so long ago that we pleaded with our mothers, "Mom, can I go out and play?" Remember? But too soon we grew up. We found that grownups often looked down upon play. They saw it as a form of idleness and a waste of time. We were encouraged to give up our childish ways, be serious and get on with mature, productive behavior. We were made to see that work was good—play was somehow unacceptable. We learned that there was something not quite right about a grown person playing.

The human need to play is a powerful one. When we ignore it we feel there is something missing in our lives and attempt to fill the void. The young husband creeps quietly behind his wife and wrestles her to the carpet, tickling her and uttering loving sounds. "What are you doing? Stop it!" she demands. "You're ruining my hairdo!"

The new wife playfully ties the bottoms of her husband's pajamas so that when he hastily tries to put them on he falls to the floor. "Very funny," he says angrily. "I thought you grew up. One would think you had better things to do." So go the playful intimacies which could bring joy and spontaneity to a loving relationship. Our adult life loses its surprise, its freedom, and we grow up seriously. Then we wonder where all the fun has gone. Perhaps it has gone with the light touch and the harmless play that was once second nature to us.

I am often accused of being childish. I prefer to interpret that as child-like. I still get wildly enthusiastic about little things. I tend to exaggerate and fantasize and embellish. I still listen to instinctual urges. I play with leaves. I skip down the street and run against the wind. I never water my garden without soaking myself. It has been after such times of joy that I have achieved my greatest creativity and produced my best work.

There is a good deal of excellent research on child's play. It has shown us conclusively that through play, with the freedom of action it allows and the stressless environment in which it occurs, children discover, relate to and define themselves and their world. It is through their play that they build their power of inquiry, vitalize themselves, and release their frustrations and negative feelings. It encourages their spontaneity, which is later responsible for their creativity. It offers them one of the few times in which they can express their personal and unique selves without outside influence. It is, therefore, paradoxical that many educators and parents still differentiate between a time for learning and a time for play without seeing the vital connection between them.

Many of us will say that we do play. We play golf, tennis, baseball, bridge, etc. But these are not play activities, they are games. They have strict rules. There are winners and losers. There are sides. There is often tension, competition, skill expectations, disappointments and criticism. I'm not saying that such games are bad. I'm merely suggesting that they are not play. In play we don't keep score. No one wins or loses. Anyone can play, alone or in a group. There are no sides—we're all on the same side.

If we make time for play, it can change our lives and it costs nothing. It has all sorts of educational, physical and psychological benefits. A happy and fulfilling adult life may even depend upon the intensity and variety of our play experiences. Of course, we will run the risk of being accused of going through our second childhood or of having lost our minds. (Where's Leo? Oh, he's out in the backyard jumping on a pile of leaves!)

It's three-thirty in the afternoon on a warm Los Angeles day. The office is especially still. The only sounds I hear are the rhythmic clicks of the typewriter and the muffled, soothing sound of someone speaking on the telephone in the next office. My eyes are heavy. My mind is dull. I'm straining to stay awake. It's the perfect time for a short nap.

I know that no one naps in the United States in the afternoon except lazy ne'er-do-wells or bums. It may be the Latin in me, but when my body cries out for rest I can't help but give in. It's comforting to know that I am joined by two-thirds of the world's population.

In Mediterranean countries, the Middle and Far East, South and Central America, Africa, everything and everyone stops for a little rest in the afternoon. Shops close, streets empty, shades are drawn and millions of civilized human beings lie down for a short period before continuing with work and the evening's recreation which follows.

The afternoon nap is not new to me. I remember that Mama and Papa would send us all to our rooms each afternoon, when it was feasible, to take a short break from the daily routine. Of course we all protested loudly, but to no avail. With their Italian heritage, Mama and Papa were never able to understand how people went eight or nine hours without a break. They knew that after a short rest they were able to work or play with more vitality.

It always amuses me to see Americans wandering aimlessly and angrily through European streets during the siesta period, waiting for the shops to reopen and cursing the inconvenience of it all. They are certain that this need to take a nap, this yielding to laziness, would never happen in the United States. It seems inconceivable to them that anyone would stop a busy, important schedule to rest in midday.

Going full steam from early morning to late evening has become part of the American work ethic. We do have all night to rest, after all. It is hammered into us from our childhood and is part of our history. Benjamin Franklin taught us, "Up, sluggard, and waste not life—in the grave we'll be sleeping enough." And somewhere in the back of our minds echoes the most sacred of business creeds that "time is money." So we continue to go against the cries of our bodies' need for rest, for getting away from it all, for regenerating, and continue to push ourselves through long uninterrupted periods of work.

I recall with amusement my first visit to Spain. Siestas begin shortly after midday and end in the early evening. At first, like so many eager travelers, I objected to spending this valuable time in my hotel room. I was restless to be on the move. But where was I to go? Museums were closed, restaurants didn't serve dinner until nine or ten o'clock, theaters opened their doors about eleven PM.

Happily (or I should say by force), I finally fell into the routine. Though I wasn't able to sleep through the entire siesta, I found that escaping the hot afternoon sun each day was a wise move, and in the cool of my room I could daydream or read or just rest for the evening ahead. I found it a splendid way to recharge from the morning's activities. I repeated this routine in Greece, Italy, Yugoslavia, Austria and even in industrious Switzerland. My parents were delighted. Leo had finally achieved a higher level of civilization! Of course, when I returned home it was back to the old rhythm. In trying to readjust, I found that I had grown accustomed to splitting up my day. So I had to become very creative to be able to set aside a short period for a nap. Sometimes I stretch out on the floor of my office, my secretary holding all calls for a short period. Sometimes I lie peacefully under a tree, often having to convince my friends that I didn't find their company boring—merely that I'd learned to obey certain signals my body was sending to my brain.

When I suggest such a routine to friends as a physical or emotional necessity, their response is predictable. "I can't nap in the afternoon, it's my busiest time." Or, "If I take a nap, it makes me groggy for hours." For some it would undoubtedly be a problem. Still, it seems to me that such a universal custom, which has existed for so long, might bear closer examination. Perhaps in time even the most active or doubting among us will see the benefits of such a proposal.

Right now I'm looking at my cat, as he curls up on a mound of wet dirt in the shade, taking his fifteenth cat nap of the day. No wonder he has lived so long and remained so agile. He knows instinctively that peak performance has its requirements.

I could continue by giving scientific proof of the value of napping, but as I said earlier, it's mid-afternoon and my eyes are getting heavier by the moment. My body is crying out for those precious moments. As Shakespeare wrote, "Oh, beloved nap time, nature's soft nurse."

A
Passion
for
Self
Respect

William James once wrote, "Probably a crab would be filled with a personal sense of outrage if it could hear us class it without apology, as a crustacean, and thus dismiss it. 'I am no such thing,' it would say; 'I am myself, myself alone.'"

The human spirit is such that it will defy every effort to lump it into categories, whether it is done for convenience or by design. It is our very uniqueness, our individual identity, that transcends our short existence here and therefore must always be preserved.

One of the most memorable characters in my boyhood was a rather eccentric gentleman known to everyone simply as Carlo. When I think of that old neighborhood, a number of characters spring to mind, but the memory of him is always a happy one. I was quite young when I first saw Carlo. He was doing what he loved best—walking in the fresh air, seemingly without direction, singing opera. Oh, how that man could sing! Arias from Puccini, Verdi and Donizetti. Sometimes he would pause for a moment, reach for a high note, and gesture dramatically to no one in particular. "He's gotta be a little coocootz," Mama would say, "but he sings good and that's-a nice." We all pretty much agreed.

Since he only performed on occasion, the novelty of hearing him sing as he did has never really worn off for me. No one ever seemed annoyed or offended. People just stared and smiled. Carlo didn't seem to mind their responses. He just moved right along, doing what, for him, came naturally.

I never knew what happened to Carlo. He just stopped coming around. Maybe he's off serenading other neighborhoods. I've always suspected that many of those who found him strange also had a secret admiration for that man. He dared to share with others what most of us, out of fear of what the neighbors would think, keep to ourselves. After all, *normal* people properly confine their bellowing to the shower. Here was an individual who followed his own joyous impulse without being too concerned with reactions that others might have.

The story carries with it a time-honored moral: You have a right to be yourself. So many of us live our lives to please others and conform to their image of us. We all have a persistent voice within that reminds us of who we are and what is right for us. There is comfort in knowing that there are people we care about who will love us even if

39

our way is a little crazy at times. What makes these people so special is the fact that they accept us in sanity and in madness. We recognize and appreciate this when we say things like, "I can be myself around him," or, "She likes me for what I am." Sooner or later we all discover that we're really not very good at being anything else. People are always saying to me, "Thank you for being you." My answer is always, "I tried for years to be someone else and it didn't work."

It seems to me that there is an implicit condition in any relationship which must suggest, "Accept me for myself or not at all. Any other arrangement is cheating both of us."

For many of us school was the place where we first learned that there were others in this world who would not accept us for ourselves. It was a hard lesson but often taught us to modify and conform. We struggled to restrain those natural impulses that set us apart from others.

Still, there is another side of us that insists upon having an identity all our own. How we love it when someone points out those special qualities that belong only to us. No finer compliment can be paid to another human being than to recognize his or her unique contribution to the rest of us which stems from being individual and special.

True, we live in a world that requires a measure of conformity. There are conventions to be respected, precedents to guide us, and some rules we must follow. What doesn't exist is enough encouragement for those of us who are struggling to be ourselves.

My value lies in the fact that I am I. Your value lies in the fact that you are you. There are those who struggle to make everyone the same. If we succumb, there will be no surprises, no laughter, no creativity, and no opera in the streets.

•   •   •

I remember quite well one of my grade school teachers who assisted me in one of my first real efforts in art. The class was supposed to draw a gold miner squatting by a stream panning for gold. The teacher began the lesson by holding up her drawing of a miner and informed us that if we followed instructions exactly, ours would look just like hers. First we drew a series of circles, then some connecting lines, then we erased here, and added there and, presto—thirty cloned miners as seen through the eyes of our teacher.

There were, as I recall, a few notable exceptions, among which was my own. My miner was fatter than the rest and had mounds of black curly hair. What made this particular memory stand out in my mind is the hurt I felt when that teacher held up my drawing to the class as an example of one who did not follow directions. The point was rather harshly made that we achieve by conforming and that individual expression was to be avoided. This teacher, who I am sure was dedicated to my growth, sought to achieve it by making a common denominator of me instead of encouraging and helping me develop that which was unique in me.

Thankfully, our philosophy of education has changed quite a bit since those days. I think we are moving away from the idea of education as mass production and more toward the idea that one of the prime elements of human uniqueness is the ability to create.

I would like to believe that everything about us is unique. There are enough forces out there that will regulate us, push us around, think for us and make us into "things," but the one counter we always have is the assertion of our unique self. Even when we were babies there was undoubtedly someone declaring that we had our mother's eyes or our father's determination or Aunt Betty's dimples—and there we lay with a face like none other, with a voice that brought a brand new sound into the world, and with a mind that would be our most unique contribution to the world.

We need to be told early and often just how special we are. We need to stop trying to make others into what we feel they *ought* to be and help them find out who they *are*. How often do we hear things such as, "Oh, it's just a stage he's going through," or, "She's a textbook case," and forget that another's experience is really unique even though it has happened before and will happen to millions of others again.

It always seems to take less energy to place people in categories than it does to know them in their own right. But when we seek out and celebrate those special qualities in others, not only do we feel closer to them, but we ourselves are enriched from the experience.

I recently talked with a woman who said to me, "I'm an ugly, unhappy, uninteresting, and lonely woman. Who can love someone like me?" I thought sadly, "Only a person seeking an ugly, unhappy, uninteresting and lonely woman."

We are almost always our own harshest critics. Very often we are the least inclined to seek out and project the positive in ourselves. It's true that our self-images largely reflect a composite of the images others have of us. If we feel unattractive or boring or inconsequential, it is primarily because we think that others perceive us in these ways. But it's also possible that they are wrong! Or perhaps we're not projecting our best selves.

This sad woman had formed a low opinion of herself and was certain others shared that opinion. She was also convinced that those who didn't surely *would* once they got to know her. Why she held herself in such low regard is difficult to say, but it was painfully obvious that her entire outlook on life, her potential as a unique human being, was stunted by her harsh perceptions of herself. Her capacity to enrich the lives of others was all but lost.

It's an old adage, but it still holds true, that if we don't like ourselves, nobody else will. Teenagers, perhaps more than others, provide ample evidence of this tendency. Many of us I'm sure can remember our adolescence. It was mostly a time of uncertainty, of changing moods, and, to varying degrees, of self-consciousness. If our hair wasn't just so, our clothes didn't fit exactly right, or a sudden blemish was on display, the whole world became an inhospitable place. Consequently we could often be found sulking in the shadows at the least assault on our self-esteem. Others might have viewed us in this context as brooding, temperamental, and unpredictable. Actually it was simply a case of momentarily not feeling good about ourselves.

Teenagers, of course, are not the only ones to succumb to feelings and behaviors reflecting self-doubt or inadequacy. It is natural that we all fall short of being the best that we can be from time to time, but to generalize these negative attitudes can be destructive and painful.

Helen Keller once wrote, "I learned that it is possible for us to create light and sound and order within us no matter what calamity may befall us in the outer world." Those of us who grapple with our self images might pause to reflect on this beautiful example of one who insisted on discovering an inner light even in the face of a darkened outer world.

Instead of viewing ourselves as defective merchandise, we should be willing to delve beyond the surface and get in touch with our uniquely-fashioned self. For as long as *we* devalue *ourselves*, so will others. We may actually begin, in time, to conform to our artificial image that can dim, perhaps for all time, our inner light.

We all feel rejected and unloved at times. Perhaps we feel momentarily out of sync with the rest of the world or that we may have less value than others. Still, we must remember that we are all that we have in the last analysis. The possibilities are unlimited if we never abandon ourselves.

If we feel ugly, keep in mind that beauty has many dimensions. If we feel unhappy, remember the words of Abe Lincoln: "Man is just about as happy as he makes up his mind to be." If we feel uninteresting, keep discovering. The world is mostly a fascinating mystery. If we feel lonely, don't wait for others to come to us—move toward others! Remember that we'll starve to death unless we exert the energy necessary to put food in our mouths.

It's not easy to give up the idea of a perfect world. We want to think of our parents as being perfect, we search for perfect relationships and perfect solutions to our problems. It is indeed a constant struggle to separate the real from the ideal—to see in our imperfection an essential element of our humanness.

We can all remember the most beloved children's stories that always seemed to end with the prince, in all his perfection and heroic, romantic, splendor, galloping off with the heroine with her virtually flawless characteristics, united for all time in their perfect love.

A currently popular theory holds that from these fantasies an indelible impression is formed of true love and happily-ever-aftering—one that persists into the realities of the adult world. There follows from this a disenchantment with real-life romance, real-life experience and real-life marriage, which are usually pale facsimiles of the perfect storybook kind.

We need sequels to these stories showing the happy couple, a little older and fatter, still contented, but just a little more reality-oriented. Children of all ages might benefit from seeing that the magic of falling in love is not lost when two people become older—even if Prince Charming is balding and his princess's backside is not as slim.

We continually indulge ourselves with the notion of human perfection, whether in individuals or in relationships. Somewhere out there, we are told, there are perfect marriages, perfect lovers, and even a perfect "10" if we look hard enough. Some of us are unfortunate enough to have grown up believing that we had perfect parents—an impression that was probably very carefully nurtured by these parents, who for some reason wished to keep their human imperfections a secret from their children. Small wonder that such children often fail at any lasting relationships, in or out of marriage, in their hopeless pursuit of the perfect life.

Our history books have long advanced the notion that our Founding Fathers were individuals of godlike perfection—perfectly moral, just, humane, etc. Only in recent years have historians searched for the persons behind the monuments. The smashing of false illusions of perfection has finally made it possible for us to truly appreciate the human being beyond the greatness, and in this way better realize our potential for the same.

Occasionally, we distinguish the imperfect in people with words such as idiosyncracy or eccentric. There are professionals who even emphasize their imperfections by drawing attention to them. When we laugh with others in this way, we are reminded not to take our own flaws too seriously and can accept the idea that imperfection is very much a part of the human condition.

Robert Clarke, in his book, *The Importance of Being Imperfect*, urges us to love our imperfect selves. "Only then," he writes, "can we afford to enjoy flawed people in peace, for we have made our peace with a flawed self; we can afford to be vulnerable in the exchange of love, for we are unafraid to give the self we love away; we can afford to become more humanity-righteous, because we no longer need to be self-righteous."

We hear it said often enough that, "I love you in spite of your imperfections," but it's probably closer to the truth to say, "I love you *because* of your imperfections."

I'd like to believe that we are by nature social creatures. Anyone who has ever experienced loneliness—and who among us hasn't—will agree with that. We need each other. But as much as we need to be with each other, we also need to be alone from time to time. The thought is expressed beautifully by Paul Tillich. In his book, *Courage To Be*, he writes, "Our language has wisely sensed the two sides of being alone. It has created the word loneliness to express the pain of being alone. And it has created the word solitude to express the glory of being alone."

One of the absolute essentials of my life is to have time to myself. Time to collect scattered thoughts, time for quiet contemplation, time to think things through, or time to just go along at my own pace. To me, it's a very reasonable demand of the body and the mind that I disengage from everything and everyone occasionally. It's amazing how often I am criticized for this trait. I, say my critics, who love people so much, have no right to be a private person.

This requirement is not new for me. I discovered it early. In my childhood there were the day-long excursions into the fields near our home, the hours of exploring whatever came into view or grasp, completely absorbed in my environment. There were very special trees that had the most accommodating branches for climbing and for building my own little fortress of solitude, way up high. When I really needed to be alone, that was my place.

I still like to break away on my own and wander to places that invite exploration. Sad to say, I'm less inclined to climb trees these days, but the stars seem just as close and glorious from the backyard porch, and it's a great deal less strenuous.

I manage to get away by myself for a few days every now and then. It's a need that reasserts itself at appropriate intervals in my life. I divorce myself from newspapers, radio, T.V., and telephone, even though it's not always easy to leave these things behind. But for me, doing this has its rewards.

First of all, there is the absolute splendor of no static from the outside. Getting far enough away from the sounds of the city means an opportunity to listen to my own heart and mind. I sometimes forget their sound in the constant roar of daily life. Having experienced this for a week or so, the renewing effect it has on my mind and body is unmistakable. Being cut off from a week's worth of news, and the calamities and carnage that are its mainstays, is a very special kind of therapy.

It's most enlightening to discover that, like a never ending soap opera, nothing is really missed by failing occasionally to keep current. In fact, separating oneself from the woes of the world can do wonders for one's outlook and general mood. One returns refreshed and optimistic!

It's so easy to become wrapped up in a routine of people and places that we neglect the all-important time of separation. Even when we find ourselves alone we are sometimes prone to fill the empty space with the chatter of a television set or a radio, almost as if we were afraid of the quiet.

We forget that there is an inner music that's nice to listen to sometimes. Thomas Edison said of his deafness that it was an asset because from it he learned to listen from within. All of us, to some degree, suffer from a different kind of deafness that is caused by ignoring or closing off those inner channels. Solitude is an excellent way of improving our hearing.

One of the most difficult things for the human mind to comprehend is that life moves on even though many of us don't seem to be fully aware of it. This lack of consciousness is often responsible for causing many of us to waste a great portion of our lives. We lose much of our childhood, our adolescence, our young adulthood, our middle age, simply because we spend so much time living in the future. The tragedy is that what is lost is gone forever. None of us has been able to relive the past or change our transgressions.

Most of us live for tomorrow. We have convinced ourselves that it will be better, that we will be richer, wiser and more secure. This may be pleasant to contemplate, but also costly if it means losing even a moment of our present. I know we are brought up to work hard, to save our money and invest in the future. In this way, we're told, someday we will be able to enjoy what we dream about. The sad part is that too often by the time we reach those golden years, we no longer need the same things or we're too tired, too ill, too set in our ways to enjoy them.

How many trips have we postponed until some indefinite time, only because they seemed too strenuous or stressful? How many possibilities of happiness have we missed because we waited for a more convenient moment? How many people have we failed to celebrate because we thought we'd have them forever?

I had a friend whose wife had always wanted to visit her relatives in Scotland, the country of her parents' birth. It was her only wish. Though they could certainly afford to go, my friend thought it was a rather frivolous way to spend money. There was always a less expensive place to go, the mortgage to be paid, the need for a new lawn mower or plans for the children's education.

Now, the house is paid for, he has his new lawn mower, the children have all been educated and are married and on their own. His wife's special dream was never realized. She died last year. He's alone with his accumulated things. It pained me to hear him lament, "I wish I had . . . ," as we so often do in hindsight.

I'm not suggesting that we should be spendthrifts or completely self-indulgent, or that we fail to plan sensibly for our future. I'm simply saying that we all have present needs and that too often they become permanent gaps in our lives when they are not realized. We all need a little frivolity and self-indulgence from time to time.

Though frowned upon in our culture, pampering ourselves now and then seems to me a healthful thing. Why should it cause us to feel a sense of selfishness and guilt, especially when these feelings take all the fun out of it? We all know the joy of buying that expensive pair of shoes we love so much, or having dinner in that elegant restaurant we read about, or sending flowers or gifts for no reason other than the special joy it will bring to someone.

It's sad to hear things such as—

"People only send me flowers when I'm ill, or in a hospital when I'm too distracted to enjoy them. And how sad that the day I receive the most flowers I won't even see them. Who needs flowers after you're dead?"

"I get presents on my birthday or the usual holidays, but I'd forego these for a surprise gift sometime—just a sign that someone is thinking about me when they don't really have to."

"We should have taken that trip last year. Now he/she is in the hospital and we may never be able to do it."

"I should have told her I loved her while she was still here."

To pass up or ignore the possibilities of present laughter, to fill our lives with plans for some nebulous tomorrow, is to court the possibility of permanent, irreparable loss. Time is limited, even for the youngest of us. It is something we can control and enhance with our expressions of love and caring now. Such opportunities come only so often in a lifetime. To suggest that we all have a right to be pampered now and again without the usual accompanying feelings of guilt is not asking so much.

We often spend our lifetime doing the sensible thing, mostly for the welfare of others. Common sense, self-denial, prudence—these things certainly have their place so long as they don't become constants in our life. We all need frequent doses of "I deserve this." Aside from what immediate happiness it brings to us, it is also a basic reminder that "I like me and I'm worth it."

A
Passion
for
Food

I, like so many of us, love to eat. It's not that I'm obsessed, for I've been known to diet and fast for days without too much trouble. It's basically that I like the tastes, the textures and the aroma of well-prepared food. I love veal and lamb and carrots and barley and beans and artichokes and asparagus and pasta and chili and corn and rabbit and chicken and chocolate chip cookies and . . . and . . . and . . .

For me, eating is also one of the last of the great rituals: we meet for a quiet lunch, we have friendly dinner parties and we linger over brunch. All of these occasions are special times when we drop the rush ethic and sit back for a few hours of sharing. Most of my happiest childhood memories are somehow connected with meals. I remember the huge piles of food on large platters, the heavenly odors, and oh, the anticipation!

Mama's minestrone soup was more than just something to eat. It became a symbol of many things. It was security, goodness, health, an economic gauge, a unifier, and an expression of love that was tangible and stuck to your ribs. Most all ethnic groups have their special soup: Chicken soup, Won Ton soup, Miso soup, Menudo, Onion are a few which come to mind.

All of us have childhood memories which refuse to die and continually cause us to relive moments of the past. One of these was the odor emanating from the soup pot. I can still see it sitting on the stove in all its enameled beauty, its contents ever-simmering, steam rising as from a dormant volcano.

When I came home from school I could pick up the aroma from the street, and when I entered the back screened porch, the odor was overwhelming. Whether Mama was standing over it with a long wooden spoon, stirring, or whether she was away from the stove, I knew that I had come home.

There is really no recipe for minestrone soup. I recall that it all started with some water and a bag of meat bones which Mama usually got free from the butcher. (He later began to charge her a few pennies for them, which she thought was outrageous.) To the bones boiling away in the water she would add vegetables: onions, tomatoes, cabbage, carrots, beans, peas, garlic (of course!)—and pastas of various shapes and sizes. I always suspected that, as with all recipes Mama cooked, there was a special secret ingredient. In this case I noticed that when the soup began to lose its flavor, or became too thick, she'd add a generous splash of wine, stir it and leave it to continue its slow, gentle simmer.

There are so many things in life which link me to my past, but few have been more lasting than Mama's soup. For my family, it became an economic indicator more ac-

curate than Wall Street. We could always judge our financial condition by the thickness of the soup. A thick brew
indicated that things were going well with the Buscaglias,
a watery soup denoted meager, less plentiful times. No
matter the abundance of food served in our home, nothing
was ever thrown out. Everything ended up in the soup
pot.

Minestrone was medicinal. It served both physical and
mental needs. No matter what time of day or night any
member of the family came home, it was soup time. If Papa
worked late—and his job as a waiter made this more often
than not—Mama would get up out of bed in her cotton
bathrobe, her long brown hair falling in waves over her
shoulders, and they'd sit down to a bowl of soup. She
mostly listened while he ate and told her of the trials and
tribulations, or joys and successes, of the day.

If we got hurt, Mama's remedy was always a Band-
Aid, a hug and a bowl of soup. It cured colds, fever, head-
aches, indigestion, heartaches and loneliness.

How often a bowl of minestrone served to unite us
and bring us together in warmth and joy! It was an act of
communion. When people dropped in, strangers included,
we would soon find ourselves huddled around the kitchen
table, talking over a bowl of steaming soup. It took care of
breakfast, a quick lunch, or a midnight snack. It was sometimes even a sign that someone needed to talk.

Mama died about ten years ago, six years before Papa.
Somehow, the house was never the same. Someone turned
the gas off under the minestrone pot the day after she was
buried, and a whole era went out with the flame.

Oh, sure, members of the family still make minestrone
soup from time to time. It's made in smaller quantities now
and only on special occasions. The continual warmth and
reassurance with which it once filled the house is somehow
missing. In fact, the younger kids say that it makes the

house smell bad, that eating it is too fattening, or that they get tired of it.

There are so few things that one can really count on these days. We need more minestrone pots in the world. I long for the security, the aroma, the taste. I'm sure there are still such soups simmering in houses all over the world.

Long may they simmer!

I'm being bombarded with the notion that we must all diet and that if we do not we'll succumb to a variety of ailments and illnesses or worse, die before our time. We are also told that skinny is beautiful, that we look best when we have a slim, sleek line. I recently attended a fashion show that was given for charity. The models all looked as if they could use a bit of the charity. Aside from the lovely faces, they appeared more like clothing racks upon which the gowns had been carefully draped.

I'm not anti-dieting and I'm very health conscious. I love my yogurt and granola and bean sprouts and wheat germ along with the healthiest of them. But I do resent the fact that I am made to feel like some sort of glutton at every meal, determined to kill myself. "You're not having another helping!" "Not that sugar-filled pastry!" "Remember cholesterol!" And so it goes.

Are we all determined to look like Jane Fonda? I like the Fonda look, but it seldom occurs to people that Ms. Fonda has a very fine bone structure. She was lucky. All of her bones are in the proper place for a classic female figure. As for the classic male, see Paul Newman or Matt Dillon. But what about those of us with larger, less classic bones? We could shake 'em and rock 'em and bounce 'em until we drop with exhaustion and still appear as if we'd had six orders of pasta in butter and a pound of Galliano cheese cake!

We seem to forget that we are not alike in many ways, and body size and shape are simply ways in which we differ. Wouldn't it be nice if we could accept this and let each other be? Still we are continually told that we must stop eating if we want all of our emotional and physical problems to end. So we starve for a few days, lose a few pounds and develop such a voracious appetite that when we give up our diet we eat everything in sight. After a day or two we're back where we started.

We very seldom ask why we are dieting. For whom are we dieting? Are we determined to make the cover of *Vogue*? Do we live for those brief moments when our friends exclaim, "Gee, you're losing weight!"? Or are we doing it for ourselves—which, in the end, is the only valid reason. I have a friend who dieted for months to please her husband, or so she thought. Her husband actually felt she looked better with the ten extra pounds!

I have friends who eat everything in sight for weeks, then pop off to the fat farm at two thousand dollars a week to lose it all. There they delight over dinners of lettuce garnished elegantly with radish and celery stick, and a small piece of mock meatloaf made with minced mushrooms. Meanwhile, their dreams are filled with Swiss chocolate and Winchell's donuts. But they stay with it. They forget that there is no law in the land that says a healthy woman cannot weigh more than 120 or a healthy man, 180.

I can't understand how people can put away enough food to keep a horse well fed and never show it, while some of us just look at a pastry shelf and gain twelve pounds. I know I must take care of my body. I want it to be the vehicle in which a healthy, productive person is housed. I love living. But I also refuse to relinquish the joy of food and the splendor of long, lovely dinners with people I care about.

I don't object to others dieting if they know why they're doing it and as long as they don't descend on me in their crusade against eating. In the end, it will matter little whether we leave this world with a size 32 or 36 waist.

It's difficult to forget painful memories of prejudice. As a child, I was one of the few first-generation Italian Americans in my elementary school. I was, of course, called a *wop* and a *dago*, accused of being part of the Mafia, and a party to the formation of a Sacco-Vanzetti radical group. All this, Papa informed me, was the usual prejudicial nonsense of the uninformed and unfeeling. I was also accused of always smelling of garlic. This, I'm certain, was true. I was raised on Allium sativum (garlic). It was strung around my neck each morning by my determined Mama over my loud protestations.

"Mama! It stinks! Americans don't tie garlic around their necks!"

"You're right," Mama would answer, with her on-target logic. "And Americans get the flu every year! You never do. So shut up!" Of course she was right. No one ever came close enough to me to spread their viruses!

When I returned from school, there were no chocolate chip cookies or cupcakes for me. I got a giant piece of Italian bread, the crust of which was rubbed generously with several cloves of garlic, then covered with butter. I loved it! I still do.

There are so many miracles in the world, miracles to be celebrated and for me, garlic is among the most deserving. You can have it whole, minced, sliced or rubbed on a salad bowl. It's high in protein, and though it is also high in calories, it has fewer than brussels sprouts.

Since ancient times, garlic has been celebrated. The Egyptians attributed God-like qualities to it. The Hebrews demanded its use under Talmudic rule. The Greeks and Romans put it into almost every dish, and especially encouraged their athletes to eat it in large quantities for strength. It's to be found to some degree in the cuisine of every nation and is often referred to as the universal herb. Over time it has been prescribed as an expectorant, a diuretic, an antiseptic and a rubefacient. It was even suggested at one time as an aid for sunstroke.

Though the founders of modern medicine, Hippocrates and Galen, all spoke highly of the attributes of garlic, it is only recently that today's medical researchers are discovering its many medical uses. They are finding that garlic may have special powers because it contains components which, when pressed or crushed, produce allyl. This acts as an antibacterial agent which seems to affect only harmful bacteria! The research seems to suggest that eating garlic is a natural way of lowering high blood pressure and cholesterol, and an aid against cold viruses, diarrhea, poor blood clotting, and rheumatism. Strange how Mama, who didn't know allyl from rubefacients and couldn't care less, knew all these things instinctively.

It doesn't really matter to me if the above research proves valuable or not. I like garlic! I never sauté anything without garlic popping away in hot olive oil. Lamb is fantastic with no other seasoning but garlic and rosemary inserted in the meat at regular intervals prior to roasting. Salad dressings come alive with garlic. There is even a delectable recipe for chicken which calls for *forty* cloves of garlic. Overwhelming! But don't be a coward. Try it. You'll love it. You need have no concern. The forty cloves are placed around the chicken in the roasting pan unpeeled.

After they're cooked they can be removed and used to season the gravy, or simply popped into your mouth as a treat for the chef. The taste is fantastic. You won't believe how mellow garlic can be after cooking.

Friends always question how a person who advocates togetherness as much as I do could suggest something as antisocial as garlic. Easy! Once eaten, garlic becomes a wonderful unifying force. People come together out of a kind of self-preservation, then stay together.

Of course I can accept the fact that there are those who, when they come within a hundred yards of garlic, turn a deep green and move away as fast as good manners will allow. No matter. I've tried to share one of life's great miracles, which is one of my major purposes in life. If there are those who don't agree, for them there may always be the miracle of parsley!

A few years ago I was told that I would live a longer and more productive life if I jogged three miles a day, gave up red meat, limited myself to four eggs a week, stopped using salt, did away with liquor of any kind, watched my diet, took food supplements and medication to lower my cholesterol count and blood pressure. Since I have a great reverence for life, I tried to do all these things. I wasn't easy but I did make some significant changes. In spite of it all, I had a heart attack that caused me to undergo a quintuple bypass operation. Happily, I recovered.

Again I was assured that exercise and diet would do the trick. Now, of course, I became more zealous than ever. I even began to read the research literature in the health journals and medical books. The result was more confusion and new anxieties; I'm certain it didn't do my blood pressure any good either.

I'm told in a series of articles by responsible doctors, for instance, that I must lower my cholesterol level because there is a direct correlation between heart disease and high cholesterol. This finding, I am assured, is conclusive, with mounting evidence being accumulated almost daily. Then I am presented with another set of studies which indicate that there is some doubt that these findings are accurate, that there is still much to learn about the cholesterol question.

I have been all but convinced that I should give up salt forever—that salt is a poison for some people. As a result I don't even have salt or a salt shaker in the house. Though I am certain that I fall into the group called salt sensitive, I am told that for most people a moderate intake of salt is no problem; and that, in fact, an absence of salt can actually be harmful.

Exercise has become another problem. The literature is full of articles and testimonies extolling the virtues of jogging, aerobics, jazzercise, and working out for the prevention of heart disease. On the other hand, I am flooded with material warning me to proceed with great caution in the area of exercise. Jogging, I am told, may put a strain on my ankles, back and heart.

In the same way, I have been convinced for years that drinking alcohol is the surest way of killing myself and to be avoided at any cost. Now I read that a glass of wine or a cocktail each evening can be a positive addition to a cardiac diet.

I have long since given up red meat. A big, juicy steak is mostly a memory for me. I have also attempted to do the same with other fatty foods and switched to a diet of fresh vegetables, nuts and beans. Now I am warned that this may not be providing me with adequate nourishment. I am also told by meat eaters that most vegetables today are sprayed with deadly pesticides and that even if they are not, some plants over the years develop natural toxins which are cancer-causing agents! (With names that would make one swear off vegetables forever.)

There's just no winning! And though most of this is beyond my humble understanding, it's enough to make me apprehensive about every morsel of food that goes into my mouth.

Of course, we've all heard that our water and air are becoming more and more polluted. Even our pure and cleansing rain is now full of acid, I'm told. So what to do? Where to turn? Whom to believe? I can't give up eating, drinking or breathing. It's enough to confuse and depress anyone who thinks about it long enough.

Good friends tell me that the best way to rid myself of these anxieties is to stop reading medical literature and start reading Agatha Christie instead. It's certainly far better than staring at my plate at every meal, wondering just what sort of chemicals and hidden toxins are lurking beneath the surface ready to do me in. I've never been a believer in "ignorance is bliss," but I might be willing to make an exception in this case.

My mother was a very wise woman. She always said, "Have it all— but in moderation." She lived to be 82. Not bad for a woman with high blood pressure and astronomical levels of cholesterol. Could it be that Mama was right again?

I've seldom seen a garden without rows of zucchini vines. I've seen gardens without Swiss chard, carrots, eggplant, and even tomatoes, but never without zucchini. Perhaps it's because they are so easy to grow and they're so hearty. They yield so much for so little energy.

Most people dismiss the zucchini as simply another

variety of summer squash. They talk about it as if it were
some sort of cucumber. But those of us who have lived
under the influence of zucchini power know better.

Papa was an expert zucchini grower. He planted them
year after year. His yield was remarkable. You could count
on it. Another thing you could count on, much to Mama's
chagrin, was that all of the zucchini was ready about the
same time. Neither Mama nor Papa were ever known to
waste a thing. Papa usually picked the zucchini daily, just
when it reached the length of his hand and the circum-
ference of a thin banana. That's the time when it was most
tender and delicious.

The problem was always how to use such a large crop
before it spoiled. Mama would steam it, fry it, can it, mash
it, put it raw into salads, make casseroles, even pickle it—
but in no way could she use all the squash which accumulated daily on her kitchen counter.

Of course, Papa's greatest joy was to share what he
had with others. I can still see him tenderly packing his
zucchini into little sacks. He always chose the best to give
away. After all, you can't give away a bruised or imperfect
zucchini. Then he'd take off into the neighborhood. We
would try to convince him that there might be some neighbors who hated zucchini. "You're crazy," he'd say. "Everybody likes zucchini!" And off he'd go, ringing doorbells
and handing over his precious gifts. Each neighbor seemed
delighted, but it was I who had to deal with the neighborhood kids who would corner me on the way home from
school. "I'll kill you," they'd threaten, "if your Dad doesn't
stop giving us those green things."

Mama, in the meantime, was kept busy giving out
recipes to neighborhood cooks.

"They're good steamed and served with a little butter
and garlic. But be sure they're not mushy—just *al dente*."

"You can egg and flour them and lightly brown them in olive oil until they're just crisp."

"You can mash them, put nuts and bits of dried fruits with them in a casserole and bake them."

"You can just cut them up and serve them raw in a salad."

"You can hollow them out and fill them with your favorite stuffing and put them in the oven."

(And all of this, please note, before Nouvelle Cuisine made the zucchini an "in" vegetable.)

Of course the neighborhood kids would have undoubtedly added their own recipe idea:

"You can throw them in the garbage can!"

It's amazing how much interchange, conversation, sharing and controversy can come from a single vegetable.

When summer was over we thought we were through with the dreaded zucchini. No way! Mama had canned quarts of it and what wasn't canned was pickled. I hardly remember a dinner where a zucchini didn't rear its green head. My sister, Lee, even gave them a special name. She called them "zucks," to rhyme with "yucks." She never dared repeat this in front of Mama or Papa, but this name brought on knowing snickers from us every time she whispered it at the table.

Yes, zucchini has real power. It's a must for any home gardener who enjoys eating it and sharing the bounty with neighbors. And did you know that as the zucchini grows it produces a beautiful yellow flower much like a lily? After you enjoy them aesthetically for a few days, and while they're still young, you can pick them for another delectable treat. All you have to do is to bread the flowers and fry them lightly in oil. They are a rare delicacy and a treat for the palate.

Others may think I'm a little crazy for singling out a mere vegetable for such a tribute, but let's face it—something so unique deserves a little praise. Long may it grow and serve!

America is having a love affair with wine. I'm delighted. Never before have so many people given up the Martini, Margarita or Gimlet for a refreshing glass of wine.

I was introduced to the magic of wine at a very young age, even before I was able to read and write. Papa always made his own wine and all of us were treated to small sips of the velvety reds and the lighthearted whites at birthday celebrations, dinner parties, Christmas, Easter, first communions and confirmations.

Of course, many in our neighborhood were shocked that we children were being given alcohol at such an early age. They were certain it would stunt our growth, fry our brains or make us alcoholics. Mama and Papa could never understand their concern. After all, it was part of the wedding feast at Cana, used at the Last Supper and offered at the communion rail. Mama advocated a taste of wine from time to time for medicinal purposes. She was certain that it was the natural way to cure anemia, liver problems, kidney ailments, and a perfect tonic to purify the blood. The privilege was, of course, never to be abused. All of us grew to normal size and none of us has a drinking problem.

The annual ritual of making the wine was one of the most festive of the year. It was planned months in advance. The grapes were ordered by the truckload and the boxes hand carried up the driveway to the garage where all the paraphernalia for grinding and pressing the grapes were stored. All the male members of the family, shirt sleeves rolled up and clothes deeply stained with purple, moved knowingly through the wine making process.

I was the smallest, so it was I who, with clean bare

feet, was put onto the pressed grapes to move them evenly around the giant barrel. While this was going on, the women were busily—and with much joy and laughter—preparing the ravioli and antipasto which would make up the dinner. What a special night! We would sit down at the table much later than usual, with voracious appetites, and devour the dinner with a passion. There was much joyful talk and endless laughter.

Papa never took wines casually. He felt it his duty to teach us all how to truly appreciate them. Never swallow wine as you do water—sip it. Never fill the wine glass so you can swish the wine about without spilling it. He informed us of the many varieties, how to appreciate the color—the rich reds, the deep ambers, the clear purples. He taught us about the nose (aroma) and how to use the mouth and tongue to sample and judge each new wine. He taught us the vocabulary that went with it—high and low acidity, corky, dull, vigorous, and so on. The experience was much like a religious ceremony—not pretentious or phony, just sheer joy, another of life's gifts to be relished.

Papa's education in wines offered me one of my greatest triumphs. When I was in my first year of college, I visited New York City for the first time. The trip was a birthday present from my more successful friends. I was taken, as part of the gift, to one of the top restaurants at the time. The name shall remain unwritten. My friends asked me to select the wine. There was an Italian wine on the list that Papa had often mentioned fondly as one of his favorites. Though it was more expensive than some of the others, I was persuaded to order it.

The wine steward was rather intimidating, with his medals and silver cup dangling from his neck. He opened the wine and poured a bit into my glass. Though Papa was 3000 miles away, I heard his instructions. Step by step I followed them carefully. I paused. Could it be? Could the wine be corky? My friends stared at me in horror. I heard Papa say, "What has been the good of so many years of preparation if you don't speak up?"

"It's corky," I stammered. "Corky!" the steward exclaimed. "We have one of the world's great wine cellars. We don't have corky wines!" I heard myself say, "Nevertheless . . . " I watched my friends cringe as the steward tasted the wine. I could hear my heart pounding wildly and wondered if everyone in the room could hear it also. My apprehension was short lived. I heard the steward whisper, "I'm sorry, sir. It is corky. You're right. I'm sorry." Triumph!

I know that there are those who, for one reason or another, will not and should not touch any alcoholic beverage. I admire them greatly for abiding by their choice. For me, a glass of wine with a good dinner will always open a storeroom of warm memories and be an occasion for celebration.

We have all been given to believe that Marco Polo brought pasta from China. I cannot tell you the times I have been put down by pseudo-historians who scoffed at my pride in Italian spaghetti assuring me that its origin wasn't even Italian! Somehow, there was something not quite right about the national food of Italy having originated in China, and in my heart I have always felt that it could not be so. You can imagine my elation recently when I learned that they were wrong. Marco Polo never made the claim of bringing pasta to Italy and historians have found that Italians were already cooking semolina flour (the stuff that pasta is made of) in boiling water as a basic food as early as 27 B.C.

You're probably wondering why I should care at all about the origin of pasta. Well, I take great pride in my Italian beginnings. Pasta has always been an important part of my life. It means a great deal to the people of Italy. It is of such importance in their daily diet that the Olympic team brought its own pasta across the sea to Los Angeles, just in case.

Most of all, a recent report by the U.S. Senate Committee on Nutrition and Human Needs has recommended that pasta be added as a daily supplement to the American diet. It seems necessary, then, that we set the record straight.

I can already see the slim-conscious among us recoiling in horror. "Pasta every day?!" they'll exclaim. "The government nutritionists have gone mad! We'll be a country of blimps and hippos." Not so! It isn't pasta that's fattening. In fact, it's very healthful. The calorie difference is between a Spaghetti Alfredo made with cream, butter and grated cheeses and a simple sauce of tomatoes simmered for hours with herbs fresh from the garden.

Is there anything more stimulating to the palate and the eye than a steaming dish of pasta covered with a sauce Bolognese heavy on the tomatoes? Primavera bright with crisp, fresh vegetables? Carbonara with prosciutto, butter and cheese? Pesto with fresh basil, garlic, cheese, pine nuts and olive oil?

There are almost as many kinds of pasta as there are ways of preparing it: thin pasta, thick pasta, tubular pasta, butterfly pasta, lasagna noodles, and on and on in every size and shape. I have just learned that Italian designer Guiliano of Turino has done a designer noodle. I can just see it in shops from Fifth Avenue to Rodeo Drive, somewhere between Louis Vuitton and Yves Saint Laurent!

Perhaps the next best thing about serving a pasta (the taste being first) is that it's so economical. For a few dollars you can stuff several dozen people. It's easy, too. Most pastas are cooked and ready to serve in 15 or 20 minutes. With a green salad or a beautiful antipasto, you have a feast.

We're so fortunate in the United States. Having developed from a cultural melting pot, the best of foreign cuisines have always been available for us to revel in—from kreplock to couscous to pickled herring to sushi to crepes to enchiladas to weinerschnitzel to fried rice to dim sum to pasta. Of course, there's nothing wrong with a great hamburger, turkey, or roast beef and potatoes; but to limit ourselves to these is sad.

So get the water boiling fast. Drop in the pasta of your choice. Wait until it's *al dente* (just a bit firm to the teeth and never allowed to get mushy). There are those who say that the best test for pasta readiness is to take a morsel out of the boiling water and throw it against the wall. If it sticks, it's done. I have never tried it that way and don't recommend it. For your wall's sake, do it the easy way—just take out a string and bite. Then toss it with your favorite sauce and sprinkle it with grated cheese (Parmesan or Romano if you can afford it, but Cheddar or Jack work well also). Pour the beverage of your choice, put Pavarotti on the record player, light the candles and go to it!

A
Passion
for
Dignity

My life was completely changed by the suicide many years ago of one of my brighter and more creative students. She left no clue, no note, no explanation as to why she should take her life. From all appearances she had everything: beauty, charm, a loving family, a promising future. But, it seems to me, somewhere along the line she must have lost sight of her own individual dignity.

Only when we realize our value as unique human beings can we begin to develop a sense of dignity and a respect for our place in life. There are so few persons giving out this message. More often than not we are dehumanized and made to feel guilty because of our differences. We become convinced that we lack what it takes to deal with life. Few encourage us to try, to risk. Too seldom are we told of our specialness or challenged with the wonder of our undiscovered selves.

I have been wondering lately whatever happened to pride. Not pride in the sense of arrogance or an exaggerated sense of self-importance, but rather a feeling of self-respect, high expectations and values relating to oneself, and a reasonable sense of one's world.

Near my office there lives an elderly man. He moves slowly, totters a bit and speaks haltingly. He lives in a small apartment house in what is otherwise an industrial center. He exists on a scandalously low fixed income. Still, he's always cheery and ready to stop anything he's doing for a neighborly greeting. He can almost always be found neatly garbed in work clothes laboring over a small garden he has planted in front of his apartment. Over the years he has created the neatest and most colorful spot in the neighborhood. It's alive with roses, azaleas, mums, or whatever the seasonal flower happens to be.

I asked him once why he worked so hard on a plot of land which wasn't even his, when his landlord seemed to care so little. "Well," he answered, "he might not care about it, but I do. I live here and it's a reflection of me. And that's enough reason." I had felt that his answer would be something like that. The other apartment dwellers love him.

This past summer I was in Switzerland. As every visitor knows, it has a long tradition of national pride. The Swiss care greatly about their country. Dozens of times I watched as people of all ages stopped to pick up litter on streets and sidewalks, or reprimand others who were abusing the environment. "This is our home," they say, "and if we want it to remain beautiful, we've got to keep our pride in it alive."

This attitude is reflected in the amount of time each household sets aside to beautify the environment with window boxes of cascading flowers, and by keeping gardens neat and manicured. They do this for themselves, not to impress the tourists. The result is a country that is a visual pleasure to experience—clean, colorful and caring. Here, in America, I look about me with sadness. I see walls and public transport smeared with graffiti. I see lovely old homes and neighborhoods abandoned to decay and often lost in overgrown weeds. Trash is often strewn on streets and sidewalks, and in public parks and recreation areas.

The attitude seems to be that anything outside one's home is not one's responsibility. It's the familiar rationalization, "If others don't feel responsible, why should I?" So we allow our public places to be converted into trash piles and we live in them. The sad part is that children who are raised without a sense of pride grow to accept, and then perpetuate, the situation. The attitude continues: "Who cares? It's none of my concern."

A friend of mine was recently planning an anniversary party. He was going over the wine list with his caterer, who suggested that he could save a substantial amount of money if he would serve an inexpensive wine. "Most people won't know the difference," he was assured. "I will," my friend replied. He wanted the best he could afford on this special occasion, to share with his friends. He paid the difference.

Too easily we judge this kind of pride as someone being a showoff. We dismiss such a person as having an excess of vanity and an exaggerated sense of importance. In reality, it may be that such an individual is making an effort which we might be simply too apathetic to make. How much easier it is to criticize in such a situation than it is to follow such an example.

When I was growing up we were very poor. I had to constantly wear hand-me-downs, often patched and visibly worn. Our home was an old frame house which had been around for years. Still, we were always immaculately clean, our clothes carefully washed and ironed. Our home was always freshly painted, the grass neatly trimmed and mowed, and surrounded by flower beds and vegetable gardens. "We don't have much," Mama told us, "but it's ours. We're proud of it and we're gonna take care of it." Heaven help us if we forgot!

I have heard from many sources that pride in oneself is not of itself a virtue. Well, that may be so. But I feel certain it's the embryo of many much-needed virtues. Long may it continue to grow.

As soon as someone wins a sweepstakes, the first thing they decide to do is quit working. To many of us, that sounds like the ideal state. Few of us realize how much happiness is dependent upon our work. We complain that we have too much work, that it's just so much drudgery, but we fail to realize that it's our work that keeps us alert, growing, and helps us to maintain our dignity.

During the recent layoffs in the automobile industry, I talked with a man who had worked all of his life. This was his first experience with idleness. At first, the newness of the situation and the requirement of receiving and reporting for unemployment compensation kept him going. But he soon discovered that the hours, days, weeks, and months of idle time were getting to him. He began to lose interest in everything, including his family. He had no incentive for getting out of bed in the morning. His life, though lacking nothing but work, seemed out of focus. Time, which he had barely been aware of before, now weighed heavily upon him. He became irritable, shouted at his children and resented his working wife.

You might say that he had everything—health, friends, a loving family, possessions and sufficient money to see him through this crisis. But there was something very seriously missing. It took time before he realized that it was the productive work that had given each day meaning. It was this realization that resulted in his throwing himself into painting the house. It saved him until he was called back to his job.

Work of any kind offers many rewards even if we don't much care for what it is we're doing. It keeps us in human company. It brings us into life. It requires us to experience new things and gives us a sense of reward. Thinking, feeling, planning have little value if we know there is no practical benefit to be gained by it.

A few years back I visited my relatives in a small provincial town in northern Italy. It was apparent what an integral part work played in their lives. Aunts, uncles, cousins—all rose at dawn and went out into the fields raking, hoeing, plowing and planting, sometimes late into the evening. There, actively moving under the warm Italian sun and over the fertile earth, there seemed to be no time for boredom. There was always something which needed doing.

In the evening, after they had washed the earth from their bodies, the festivities began. Good fresh food from the garden, cool wines from the cellar, animated conversation, laughter, joking, teasing and general rejoicing. Before too long they were all peacefully sleeping, ready for the next day's work.

I realize that many would ask, "Is that enough?" For some, perhaps not. But I never saw such smiles. Their lives had meaning, and at the heart of it was work and the rewards they received from it. They knew a congenial occupation, something into which they could enter with abandon, which offered them emotional and physical peace.

I know that there are many who criticize and come down brutally hard on the Puritan ethic that has made work such a vital part of our mentality. They will point out that for many, work is dull, demeaning and offers no greater reward than a small paycheck at the end of the week. They will argue that there is little good that can be said for time spent at a job which we abhor, and of course I would agree. But these situations may also serve as an incentive for bettering ourselves and our skills.

We have all had many jobs—some routine and others challenging. We know that work, well done, is rewarding and even necessary for human well-being. Our lives change when we stop looking at our work as a necessary evil and begin to see it as a privilege. We may then start executing it with more gusto, excitement and dignity.

I recently watched some World War II footage on television which showed several military men being honored with medals for various feats of valor. It was all very impressive. Amid the cheering crowds and fanfare were heads of state and generals pinning on the medals and, in some cases, even kissing the recipients on both cheeks. One man was being recognized for having risked his life to save his buddies. Another one was honored for having blown up tanks or downed enemy planes.

We love to pay tribute to our heroes, perhaps for what it inspires in all of us—to reach above and beyond the everyday pattern. Certainly, I'd not be the one to deny anyone his medal, but suddenly it occurred to me that there are so many who deserve recognition for what they do, but who will more than likely never get it —no medal for distinguished service, no Pulitzer prize, no Nobel prize, no public recognition.

Medals should go to parents who successfully raise children through teething, tantrums, braces and broken hearts, and all the growing pains in between—and in spite of it continue to love them without expectation or reward.

I'd like to bestow an award on grandparents who, after years of giving of themselves, are not content to live their lives in their children's shadows, but continue to grow and work independently and enthusiastically.

I'd like to reward all the political leaders who are sincerely engaged in the endless struggle for a better quality of life for us all.

Likewise, I'd like to give a medal to the professionals in our society who maintain their ideals, practice their skills with pride and dedication toward a healthier, more sane, more livable society.

Recognition would be no less deserved for our blue-collar workers who help keep our cities safe, clean, and running efficiently, whose work we all take so much for granted, and without whose daily contribution we would surely fall apart.

I would like to give medals to educators who, despite low salaries, difficult classroom conditions, and often low public esteem, continue to educate our young people year after year and, for the most part, succeed.

I would like to single out researchers in all fields who spend most of their time in laboratories, with little or no financial support, seeking secrets with patient devotion—secrets which will enhance life and human well-being.

There are so many artists, writers, musicians, singers, and entertainers of all sorts who deserve medals for the hours of joy, inspiration and beauty their creativity brings to all of us.

All of the these people make our society work and they should be recognized for it.

Of course, we know that there are less than ideal parents and grandparents, as well as dishonest and self-serving politicians, teachers, public servants and professionals. Strangely enough, they are the ones we seem to notice the most, often to the extent that we lose sight of or take for granted the good that the majority does.

Most of the latter will never appear on television or in newspaper headlines. Very few of them will ever receive medals. In fact, they never expect them. Still, I think it's a great idea and I guess it's up to us to find the means of honoring each other.

It doesn't take much—an encouraging, complimentary word to a good mother, father, an honest professional, fine teacher, or to a hard-working fire fighter or policeman. I don't think they'd care so much about a formal ceremony. A simple expression of thanks, a positive gesture or a brief telephone call can have great value, also.

Aristotle wisely made an important distinction when he wrote, "Dignity does not consist in possessing honors, but in deserving them." Good work and steady devotion to one's principles do have their own rewards, but a little recognition now and then certainly doesn't hurt.

I saw a futuristic movie that gave another one of those bleak accounts of life in the 23rd century. There was hopelessness everywhere; lives were lived mechanically against the background of a sterile and colorless, often violent, world. People were vacant, pressed into a painful uniformity and seemingly without personality.

There have been a number of books and films in recent years that give a similarly bleak account of the future. It's interesting how they share this stark vision of tomorrow. One supposes that it's based on an appraisal of the present—that authors feel we are, in fact, headed down such a road now. Depersonalization, they suggest, seems to be one factor that points us in that direction, because it has become more and more a part of our present.

I have a friend who regularly points out the grim and unmistakable signs of our dehumanization. He loves to use the government as an example. "We're nothing more than an index card or a speck on some microchip," he tells me. "We're a statistic that gets counted and catalogued every 10 years, and only noticed when we fail to pay our taxes."

He recalls when there was a bond between producers and consumers. Then quality and reputation meant something, when people were more important than profit. There is, no doubt, some truth in his observations. There are times when all of us feel swept up in a mass culture; a modern society that places increasingly less emphasis on person-to-person intimacy. Perhaps it is part of our love/hate relationship with a technology that takes us to the limits of our imaginations, but often abandons us there, to feel more isolated than ever.

My friend works in an office where he spends the better part of his day inside a cubicle with a computer. His daily regimen is imposed upon him by his machine; he is supervised by it, even disciplined by it. His interaction with other people at work is pretty much confined to coffee and lunch breaks. Under these circumstances, one can understand his feeling of alienation.

But I believe he is more the exception than the rule. It seems to me that companies and corporations that employ people in repetitive and tedious work, especially work that is done in isolation, have, more than ever, rediscovered the importance of meeting human needs. They've learned that people who are made to feel less like people don't perform well in any kind of work situation. They acquire attitudes of apathy and boredom. They develop ulcers and nervous habits. They're more often ill, need medical attention more frequently; they tend to burn out earlier.

It's very simple. We need each other. In our day-to-day living there is no substitute for the human touch. We need other people to appreciate our accomplishments and encourage our creativity. No matter how much we automate our lives or learn to substitute wires and circuits for people, that message is clear.

At the supermarket, a checker told me that her job will soon be automated. "I won't be needed at all," she sighed. I tried to reassure her that her friendly smile and warmth were irreplaceable, but she seemed resigned to giving way to speed and efficiency. I certainly hope she's wrong.

In 1970, Alvin Toffler wrote *Future Shock*. In this book, he talked about how we were becoming a modular society. He warned about people in our lives whom we treat like components—plugging them in and out to suit our needs. He used the example of a modular shoe salesman: "Consciously or not," he said, "we define our relationships with most people in functional terms. So long as we do not become involved with the shoe salesman's problems or his more general hopes, dreams and frustrations, he is fully interchangeable with any other salesman of equal competence."

I am not afraid of the implication that people will become replaceable or are indeed interchangeable. I am certain that however great are the changes in store for our future, the human being will triumph. But in working to build a better future, that is something we cannot afford to take for granted.

A Passion for Plants and Animals

I was astounded to read that Americans own somewhere around one trillion pets. That's TRILLION, not billion. I suppose that number includes hamsters, guppies, bunnies and the like. Still, we are second to none in our consuming interest in maintaining animals in our domestic environments. There have been some very interesting studies recently about pets and plants and the effect they have on their owners in terms of stress reduction, lowering blood pressure and even of lengthening their lives. Researchers have discovered that patients who nurture pets and plants actually have a more successful rate of recovery from illnesses and disease than those without them. It seems that they tap a nurturing instinct that is life-enhancing and common to us all.

I realize that coming home from a hectic workday and sitting down to look at your fish or pet turtle (instead of more traditional ways of relaxing) may sound pretty crazy. But experiments have shown that different interactions between pet and owner can be quite therapeutic. The intimacy of petting, stroking, hugging, even talking to an animal, for instance, has measurable effects on blood pressure and stress reduction. The unconditional love which seems to be so difficult to find among humans appears to be automatic with pets. In addition, they inspire our more playful nature. They make us laugh.

I'm not suggesting that these things are available to us only through our association with the animal kingdom. Anyone who has ever spent a sleepless night listening to the howling and screeching of neighborhood pets might want to argue the point vigorously, especially about animals and stress reduction. I do find it interesting, though, that what we sometimes observe in animal behavior is what we would like to see in humans.

It's not often that we find a person who will love us without regard to age, fortune or physical condition. How many people always greet us with enthusiasm and are acutely sensitive to our moods? Small wonder that we often treat our pets like people, sometimes even better. I know of a certain poodle that is fed only the choicest cuts of beef (cooked medium rare), has its own wardrobe, a birthday party once a year with cake and only pedigreed guests in attendance, and even has a prepaid plot in a local pet cemetery.

There are obedience schools that issue diplomas to dogs wearing mortar boards on their heads during the graduation ceremony. Some churches will bless your animal, while one in California even performs marriage ceremonies for pets that have mating on their minds. And isn't it interesting how we have become to a degree desensitized to T.V. violence and torture where people are involved, but when an animal is in any way victimized, become indignant and write letters of protest.

I don't pretend to know much about animal behavior—I'm still too puzzled by the human kind. I do have my cat, Cocktail, and between us there is a sort of understanding. We're both very independent creatures who need a place to call home and the freedom to get away once in a while. He likes his catnip and I like my California Chardonnay '82. We both like classical music and dislike visits to the doctor/veterinarian.

Quite frankly, I've never really thought of my cat in any therapeutic sense. He does make me laugh sometimes when he falls on his back, legs in the air, and snoozes in the warm sun. I'm sure he thinks I'm funny too.

If raising and caring for pets helps us learn how to be more loving and caring friends, lovers, parents, etc., then we are fortunate in having them. If they put us more in touch with all living things and our responsibilities to tend to them carefully and lovingly, then we can indeed be thankful that trillions of them are around.

I know that everybody thinks their dog or cat is the most beautiful, has the most wonderful personality, or is the most intelligent. Well, let me tell you about mine. He doesn't have pedigree papers but he's certainly not just an ordinary alley cat. He appeared at my doorstep one rainy night—frightened, hungry, alone and wet. He couldn't have been more than three inches from the ground—a tiny pack of bones. (No way did I imagine that he would grow to be the size and weight of a baby hippopotamus.) At any rate, from his first pleading meow, though I had many times sworn that my busy schedule was not conducive to pets, I knew he was mine.

After a good feeding, I examined him carefully: lovely gray coat, large green eyes, perky ears and a cocked tail. His name came easily—Cocktail (no reference to the gin and tonic variety).

It soon became apparent that Cocktail was no ordinary cat. Yes, he had the usual traits: independence, a certain aloofness, a natural knowledge of human frailty. But there was something more—something deeper, mystical, all-knowing. My friends called it *cat psychosis*, but Cocktail and I knew differently.

One day I was looking through a psychological journal and found an interesting classified ad. It stated that a researcher was seeking cats who seemed to have behavior patterns which revealed the possibility of high intelligence. He was in the process of creating and standardizing a cat I.Q. test.

Always eager to aid in the advancement of science, I answered the ad. Within a few days I received a box containing a ball, a string, a bell, a pencil and an instruction sheet. I could hardly wait to begin the experiment. Of course Cocktail had his own ideas and it wasn't until a week or so later that he wandered over to me, ready for the game.

Each item was scored according to function such as approach, activity, planning, execution, attention span and so on. For instance, when you rolled the ball to the cat, did he play with it? How did he play with it? Did he lose interest after a moment or did he remain with the task at hand? Did he retrieve the ball? Did he seem to enjoy the game?

These activities, plus general traits, were written on the scoring sheet and put into a self-addressed envelope to go to the researcher. A response was promised shortly.

Cocktail didn't object to the many activities. In fact he seemed intrigued with the attention and the diversity of the problems presented to him. I must admit, I lost interest before he did. The test included a questionnaire that I found rather disturbing. It asked, "Does your cat recognize you as its keeper and choose to come to you rather than others in a group?" I couldn't honestly say that Cocktail selected me particularly out of a group. In fact, it seemed as though he selected that person most allergic to cats. Does that mean he is wise? nasty? intuitive? or what?

After a few weeks I received an excited letter from the experimenter. Cocktail had the highest I.Q. score of any cat tested so far—a cat genius!

It's not easy living with a genius—even a cat genius! There is no way of knowing what he's thinking, what he's about to do or when he'll do it. Cocktail seemed to sense the triumph. He seems to move with more grace, spends more time preening himself and eats only the more expensive cat foods.

We spend millions of dollars each year on cat food, vets and flea collars. Our cats are oblivious to their expense. They reject a mackerel dinner with the flippancy of a princess abandoning paté with truffles. They do what they want when they want and are ready to scratch you without a qualm if you interfere with their needs. Still, we love them, care for them, worry about them, plan their food and take them to the vet at any sign of a disorder. It's a cat's life, indeed!

Cocktail is sitting on an embroidered pillow I picked up in Korea and to which, over my protestations, he's become attached. He is partially awake, knowing, I'm certain, that I'm writing about him, but feigning total disinterest.

Sometimes I wonder who needs the I.Q. test!

• • •

It took me a long time to understand Papa's enthusiasm for growing things. Not until I was on my own did I find any satisfaction in scattering a few seeds and watching them grow. But I still remember Papa's excitement every spring, anticipating a new crop of flowers in the backyard. Actually I regarded it as some sort of seasonal madness that overtook him. What else could account for working fertilizer into the soil with such elation?

It was just a small suburban plot that we had then, but Papa always made use of every square inch of it. He was continually going outside to look things over. He'd pull a few weeds between the corn stalks, give a little support to the peas, and gently pat the zucchini vines, pleased to be a part of it all. Papa was a true nurturer. Not a year went by that he didn't cultivate that little patch. He used to bring me out and show me, with great enthusiasm, when the seeds first broke through the soil.

"You see what a miracle this is, Felice?" he would exclaim. "You get so much with just a little care and love." For my part, however, knowing that a small green speck would in time grow into a cauliflower was hardly my idea of a miracle. Still, I'd muster my enthusiasm and humor him with, "Yes, Papa. It's wonderful!" Later I would come to understand.

Papa fully agreed with Luther Burbank, who said that, "Love is the secret to improved plant breeding." It's quite an amazing statement from a man of science, but devoted gardeners, indoor and outdoor, know it to be true. It's only part of another truth which says that all life, not only human, is affected positively by love.

It has become fairly well accepted now that, like human beings, plants respond to the warmth of the human voice, have feelings, can sense moods, and may even have musical preferences. Perhaps the reason I don't have too much luck with house plants is that they don't like my music. A constant dose of opera, after all, is not everyone's cup of tea. Puccini and Richard Strauss and Wagner may admittedly get the best plant down.

We have developed plant hotels and plant sitters, both available to offer care and company when we are away. There are plant doctors and even plant psychiatrists, I am told, for the really temperamental types. There are plant probes that can be inserted into the soil and actually hum when conditions are just right. My favorite is a plant stand that says, "Thank you," whenever you tend to the plant that sits on it.

There is some interesting work being done right now in mental institutions and drug rehabilitation centers. Patients are being given seeds or small cuttings of plants and encouraged to tend them. It is their plant; and its well-being, in fact its very survival, is in their hands. The results from these studies have been quite exciting and very positive. Whatever the reasons, these activities seem to bring meaning back into otherwise confused lives. It also brings a sense of creation, a sense of having accomplished something positive and good, and the reinforcement which comes from the knowledge of a job well done. This same finding has been supported among the elderly in convalescent homes. Nurturing seems to tap essential feelings of dignity and inner peace.

I have friends who have pots of African violets in every room of their house. Regardless of their setting, they seem to flourish. They develop gigantic, rich green leaves and an assortment of strikingly colorful blooms. I have never seen the likes of them anywhere else. I continually ask my friends for their secret. Their answer is always simply and matter-of-factly the same: "Just water, a little light and some love." The statement is more profound than it sounds.

Plants ask for little more than light, water, fertilizer,

and some kind attention now and then. Perhaps people ask for a bit more, but the dynamics are essentially the same, whether it is a prize-winning squash, a little pot of grape ivy, or a human being. In fact, it may be one of the answers to the question of what life is all about.

A
Passion
for
Change

The human mind is a miracle. Once it accepts a new idea or learns a new fact, it stretches forever and never goes back to its original dimension. It is limitless. No one has even guessed its potential. Still, so many of us spend a lifetime marking boundaries and defining limits. Young children in their innocence have not yet learned their limitations and so joyfully and instinctively stretch to learn, and so should we all!

I remember a wooden plaque that hung on the kitchen wall in the house where I grew up. A simple proverb in Italian imparted the wisdom of the world in capsule form: "Siamo vecchie troppo presto, e troppo tarde intellengente." (We get too soon old and too late smart.) It wasn't until much later in life that I allowed the significance of that familiar message to settle in my mind. It reminded me that a human life is indeed short, especially when we attempt to reach its full potential. It told me that each moment of our lives was essential in bringing us closer to realizing that potential. Yet to arrive near the end only to reflect on how much was missed along the way is one of the greatest of human tragedies.

Each day we should learn something new about the world, and in so doing we will never again be the same. If we feel inconsequential or that our lives are becoming stagnant, we should celebrate the limitless capacity we have to experience more.

To place proper value on learning, we need to recognize a basic law of nature: *That which does not grow, dies.* Children who watch television for six hours a day (which is the norm) will probably develop a passive attitude toward their world. Indoors, they will miss the birth of spring or the first soft snows of winter. A life that is lived within fixed limits and that travels only the well worn paths of habit and routine is diminished greatly by failing to recognize that we live in a constant state of change. *That which does not grow, dies.*

We often grow up to comments such as, "I had to learn this, so will *you*," with the flip side being, "If it was good enough for *me*, it's good enough for *you*." Adults often adopt this line of reasoning when they must confront the whys and wherefores of children. In the process they deny them their precious need to know. Think of the possibilities for learning when we say to another, "I don't know the answer but let's find out together. Together we can unravel some of the mystery and explore the wonder that is everywhere about us."

Too many of us settle on the notion that education is something that took place at a fixed period in our lives. We mistakenly classify people's intelligence according to the number of years that they attended school. Rather we should regard education as a never ending pursuit and see that the truest measure of intelligence is a dedication to continue the process throughout life. Some of the most ignorant people I know have advanced degrees to show for their education while some of the wisest people I know never made it past high school. It's not really a paradox if we keep in mind that learning is not confined to a classroom and is not imparted solely by people whom we designate as teachers. We are all teachers and we are all students. I believe that it is the mark of true wisdom to appreciate and profit from both roles.

Each day is a fresh beginning, a little life unto itself. Most of us have struggled to live up to this moment, to come to this time. Opportunities for growth, a chance to learn something new—some things in life come along only once, and it is our choice alone whether we seize them or not.

The old advertising slogan, "So simple a child can do it," has taken on new meaning for me.

For a long while I've been intimidated by the specter of a computerized world. Everyone tells me how simple computers are. I've been to seminars showing me the unbelievable time-saving possibilities of these electronic marvels. They are especially helpful, I am told, for anyone who writes as much as I do. I can no longer fight this fact. I know that it's true; I've seen it work. They use little space and can do things in moments which require me, a pair of scissors, and a roll of tape, many hours to accomplish.

I am not fighting against our entry into the computer age. Far be it for me to resist the inevitable. The future is here and it comes equipped with a keyboard, a key pad, a viewing screen and a printout.

The fact is that the future arrived in my office a few weeks ago. There is now a personal computer sitting on the table where I used to spread out my legal pad and pens. (I should add that I am advanced enough to use a felt tip pen, not a quill.) My secretary operates the new machine. She has taken to it like an Italian baby to spaghetti. I stand over her shoulder marveling, as if she were doing sleight of hand or card tricks.

Since this computer is here and ready to be used, or, ready to be accessed, as they say in the computer world, I thought it wise to make use of its fullest potential. But how do I get access to this marvel, since anything more complicated than a dependable old wall-mounted pencil sharpener exposes my mechanical illiteracy?

I know that children have no fear of the future, so that seemed a good place to seek help. I have a nephew, Ronald, in elementary school, who has a near total mastery of anything mechanical, and this includes computers. I told him this thing was in the office and I needed help.

"Does it have a dual disc drive?" he asked without hesitation. "They're better if they're built in." I was unable to answer him, not knowing what a disc is, let alone whether my new acquisition has one. He produced a box of floppy discs from his room. I recognized that the computer in my office does indeed have slots for them.

We continued to discuss, in somewhat mystical language, my system. When I asked if it would be possible for the computer to do certain things, I was corrected.

"Computers don't 'do things'; they 'perform functions,'" he said. "They don't 'hook up' to other computers; they 'interface.' You don't call it 'that little thing with the two cups that the phone fastens to,' the proper term is 'modem.'"

I had no difficulty being tutored by my twelve-year-old nephew. He never spoke condescendingly to me. He took the machine for granted and has simply accepted the fact that computers are now a way of life. He plays with them and does his homework on them and even creates programs for them.

I, on the other hand, am awed by what this equipment can do. It can interchange paragraphs, switch words around and even correct my spelling. It informs me of its limitations, takes commands and asks questions. It even seems to have a sense of diplomacy. Rather than accuse me of making an error, it prints "One of us has made a mistake!" It never gets tired and is always patient and ready to go when I am.

I think it was somewhat normal for me to be leery of computers. They represent a break with some very familiar habits and traditions. It is only human to instinctively avoid anything that shifts radically from the acceptable, comfortable past. But the world is governed by ceaseless change and we must therefore establish links with the present and future as well as the past. Computer technology is an excellent case in point, as the newest systems grow obsolete in only a few years, or even months.

This ability to see, experience and accept the new is one of our saving characteristics. To be fearful of tomorrow, to close ourselves to possibilities, to resist the inevitable, to advocate standing still when all else is moving forward, is to lose touch. If we accept the new with joy and wonder, we can move gracefully into each tomorrow. More often than not, the children shall lead us.

• • •

I was recently introduced to one of those talking cars—
the ones that have little recorded messages for people: "Excuse me but you forgot to close the door completely."
"Turn off the lights, please." "Oh! Oh! You've left the key
in the ignition." When I first heard of this innovation, I
remember shaking my head in amazement and wondering,
"What next?" Of course, I wouldn't mind a car that would
slip in an occasional "Hi, Leo, you look terrific today!"

It's interesting how we sometimes approach, with
mixed emotions, the benefits of modern technology. Instinct makes us a little cautious in the face of change, especially when it threatens our established traditions or habits. Take watches, for example. The fact that my friend's
multi-function digital watch tells time is not nearly as important to him as the thrill of the intergallactic war game
that it includes and he can play whenever he's bored. On
the other hand, they tell me that in the not-too-distant
future our wrist watches will be minicenters of communication, receiving televised transmissions, even serving
as telephones.

There are predictions that we will become more visual
and less verbal in the coming century. Video discs will
supposedly replace books to a large extent. My first reaction to that is NEVER. It conjures a vision of our libraries
being converted into learning arcades with people somehow electronically wired, each in his or her own little cubicle. I suppose in each of us there is an irrepressible tra-
ditionalist. But I also remember from a history lesson long
ago that Gutenberg's invention of movable type was met
with great resistance because it threatened the tradition of
orally passing along information and telling stories.

Medical advances promise to extend lives well beyond
present expectancies; and, of course, this raises many questions for us all. As with any revolutionary change in hu-

mankind, there is a fear of tampering with natural order. Caroline Bird in her book, *The Good Years*, sees something positive in the wealth of resources which a large population of older people would bring. She writes, "They will become the innovators, drawing on their lengthening historical perspective to see a wider canvas of the human experience."

It's truly difficult to keep a perspective when we deal with the unknown. But again, it's helpful to draw from past experience to judge more reasonably where the future is leading us. The Wright brothers were told repeatedly that if God had intended men to fly, He would have given them wings. Only sixty years later, men were walking on the moon.

I'll always be skeptical of the idea that in any aspect of our lives we will require less human contact—all technological innovations to the contrary. Case in point: A few years ago a good friend received one of those questionnaires from a computer dating service. "Just fill it out and send it in and we'll get back to you," it said. He decided that a little experiment was in order.

He was not exactly truthful in his answers. In fact, he made himself sound more like Attila the Hun or Jack the Ripper than a prospective date. He did this only to see if a computer could find a match for the completely unlovable person he invented. He was not surprised, but a little wary, when a reply came within days informing him of the dozens of individuals on the computer's compatibility index who were possibly right for him!

I know that computer dating has indeed helped bring people together, but being the hopeless romantic that I am, I'm more inclined to believe that the real magic still lies in two people personally discovering each other and not in the mating of two data processing cards.

I don't believe that modern technology is somehow

foreclosing on our humanity. It's comforting to know that there are human constants like truth, beauty, love, laughter—so many complex and also amazingly simple aspects of our makeup that will always be irreplaceable because they will always be uniquely human.

The only certitudes I've found in life are death and change. One is an end, the other a beginning. Change is life. Without change there would be no growth, no understanding, no relating and no surprises. We are by nature changing beings. Still, we seem to fear and resist it more than any other aspect of life.

Healthy human beings welcome the opportunity to adapt to new experiences. In fact they're quite comfortable in a constant state of change. They are alive to the possibility of becoming someone new each moment. Only habit and apathy prevent the rest of us from having the same outlook.

When we don't care, or resign ourselves to patterns and routines, we begin to stagnate. We are prone to accept the comfortable illusion that life is a series of habits and conditioned responses. In actuality this is a comfort more like a disease, which leads to a kind of intellectual and emotional death. We can allow ourselves and a dynamic world to go to waste. Ellen Glasgow, an American novelist, said, "The only difference between a rut and a grave are their dimensions."

To accept new ideas and give up old values and habits is not always comfortable. It is often easier for us to deny that there may be more appropriate, more creative possibilities for our lives. We fail to understand that when we resist these potentialities, life becomes at best a continual struggle; at worst, it passes us by and we are left alone and lonely.

We constantly hear that there are people who will never change, that they can't change for one reason or another. It's a familiar litany and utter nonsense! Change is always possible unless our brain has stopped functioning. It is a choice that need not be wrenching or threatening. Adapting to life's currents is a natural process, and, in the final analysis, the path of least resistance.

A few years ago my next door neighbor, who was in his seventies, was served an ultimatum by his children: his desire to find a new life after the death of his wife of many years was an impossible dream and must be abandoned. "You're too old and set in your ways to change now," they told him. Perhaps they felt it was time for him to collect his memories instead of charging ahead to make new ones. Happily he was wise enough not to listen. His family was shocked when they heard that he had gone dancing at the local recreation center. They were appalled when he met a lovely lady and decided to remarry! "There's no fool like an old fool—you're going to know nothing but misery," they all told him. This man died three happy years later while on a wonderful trip to New York, a city he'd never seen but always wanted to. He fell peacefully, smiling, into the arms of his new wife.

Of course the new, the untested, the uncertain cause their share of anxiety. But any change is better than none and most change is for the better. It has the power to uplift, to heal, to stimulate, surprise, open new doors, bring fresh experience and create excitement in life. It elevates us from mediocrity and saves us from false security. Certainly it is worth the risk! We must also keep in mind that it is only through change that we can continue to experiment with ourselves and our lives.

Change also causes us to alter our perceptions so that

we are never locked into our opinions and feelings about each other. We may find that cousin Fred, who has always been a crashing bore, or our neighbor who is standoffish, are one day changed. Or perhaps it is *we* who are changed in how we perceive them.

When we find that life is a bore, that existence is a chore, that the wonder and magic of being alive is vanishing, it is possible that it is because we are resisting change. If we have become trapped in a dull, lifeless rhythm, we must resolve to give up our resistance and dance to a new step. When we do, we will surely rediscover that change is our greatest source of happiness, stimulation and continued growth.

A
Passion
for
Overcoming
Frustration

Of all the living creatures in our world, only humans accumulate problems and wear them like a yoke around their necks. Some of us even have a remarkable facility for embracing the frustrations of others. We love making other people's frustrations ours! As if our own were not enough! There is no question that conflict does darken the world around us, and it is entirely human to recognize and try to avoid it. But in meeting conflict, we need to understand that the process doesn't end once we solve a problem; there will be more ahead. The positive aspect of this is that in those experiences there also exists great potential for growth.

My car sometimes decides to make noises, but only for my ears. When I become fearful that it will fall to pieces, I take it in to be checked. I tell the mechanic about the problem and we listen together. Magically, the noises disappear. So we take it for a spin around the block and it purrs more quietly than on the day I bought it. I make an utter fool of myself trying to recreate the noise and assure him it's real. The mechanic scratches his head and says he has never heard any such sound. So I leave and there is the noise again!

Phones are also sources of frustration. I am constantly getting busy signals. If I do get through, I'm put on hold or get that tinny sound of piped-in music which drives me mad. After five songs someone comes on the line and asks, "Are you being helped?" "What can I do for you?" I re-explain what I want. "I'll put you through," they say, and in an instant there is an emptiness and silence—we've been disconnected. I redial and go through the whole process again. This time I'm informed that I need to be transferred to another department. Back we go to the switchboard operator, who directs me to someone else. Now I get another chance to tell my story. Of course, this is only the third time.

The very ultimate in frustration for me comes in the form of instruction manuals. I try to avoid them, but once a year or so I'll get something that comes in a box with two of the most dreaded words in the English language written on it: Assembly Required.

Nothing can reduce me to a jibbering idiot faster than a set of instructions with a bunch of parts, cryptic diagrams, and a jargon that defies rational explanation. For example: "Insert rocker arm assembly over carriage bolt while releasing preset selector wheel (See Figure A)." Inevitably, at the end of the whole operation, I discover an extra part, or worse—a part is missing, which tells me that this thing that I've put together is going to be defective; it's going to shake or fall apart and do something it shouldn't.

While I'm on the subject of frustrations, why is it that every time I open the utensil drawer, the first thing I see is the nutcracker? That is, until I want to crack a nut—then it has gone into hiding. And why is it that the section of the newspaper I most want to read has crash landed in the shrubbery where it's torn or wet beyond salvation?

And what about when the dessert cart is wheeled over to your table at a restaurant and you see desserts that were made in heaven but you know that one more bite will bring on indigestion. Of course, you order it anyway. Who can resist? And you spend the rest of the night reading a book because of that one additional bite.

Does anyone else feel these frustrations or is it that I am more neurotic than most? I only know it makes me feel better when I air them out, and especially when I find that other people feel them too. In fact, they will often share very helpful suggestions for coping that I hadn't thought of.

For instance, it was suggested that I take the dictionary and learn a new word when I'm put on telephone hold. Someone else suggested that for an extra few dollars most stores will assemble items which need putting together. The dessert problem can be solved by looking at the dessert cart before ordering dinner and planning accordingly.

It's nice to learn that I am among millions who share petty frustrations. We all have them. They are as much a part of life as death and taxes. It does us good to recognize them for what they are, have a good laugh and let them go. When we do, they seem to fall into perspective. After all, I know it's frustrating, but what other choice is there?

•   •   •

I don't know about you, but I can't throw anything away. I still have neckties that are five inches wide and sport coats with one inch lapels. I have term papers I wrote in elementary school on the effects of the Industrial Revolution, and postcards I received from Aunt Pina when she visited Venice, Italy, in 1940.

I keep promising myself that I am going to have a monumental cleaning one day and get rid of it all. But just as I get about doing it I start feeling the romantic pangs which I attach to these inanimate objects. My memories give them heart and in no way can I throw out things of the heart.

My mother gave me that tie on my twentieth birthday. I traveled around the world in those pants. That term paper was my first truly researched literary masterpiece. Perhaps someday someone will reprint it as part of a biography: Leo—The Early Years. So the boxes get more plentiful, the bags take up more space and the house gets smaller. I even have cancelled checks and income tax forms from 1942.

When I was deeply involved in the study of Zen, I remember that my teachers had nothing more than the clothes on their backs and a small bag full of their belongings which they flung over their shoulders. In a few moments they could pack and be off, free to roam where they willed. I can't imagine what I'd do if an emergency made it essential that I leave my home. How many moving vans would I require?

I know people who rent space in order to store possessions for which there is no longer any room in their house. They have the crystal they were given on their wedding day still neatly and safely packed in its original box. They are even saving the white ribbons. They are stored next to the bone china which they have never used. They are not quite sure what they are saving these things for, or why. They just sit there. I am certain that heaven supplies its own crystal and bone china. It doesn't need the few pieces they've been saving for so many years.

We are part of a society that loves obsolescence. We never totally wear things out. We just store them somewhere. After all, we say, it's still good and we may need it someday. If we keep it long enough, we rationalize, it may even be worth a great deal of money as an antique! We collect used pipe, odd pieces of rugs, battered suitcases, broken ironing boards, picture frames, old 45 and 78 rpm records—you name it, there's a collector for it.

Philosophers for centuries have reminded us of the uselessness of collecting. They have warned us, as Buddha did, that the more we have, the more we have to worry about. I have never seen a statue or painting of Jesus of Nazareth, Lao Tzu, or Buddha with mounds of travel gear, or carrying huge packs of belongings. It is always we simple humans who have loaded elephants, camel trains, or trucks.

As time passes we often become the slave of our things. We are fearful of taking a holiday because we're concerned about our belongings being left alone. A friend has a new Mercedes which he never parks in a parking lot or on a crowded street for fear of someone scratching it. But he is equally worried about leaving it on a side street for fear that it will be stolen. It's interesting to ponder whether he owns the car or the car owns him. But we are all in some way as guilty as he.

I wish I had a solution to the disease, but it just seems to get worse. The more we have, the more we seem to want and need, and the more we have to be concerned about.

A poet, D. Johnson, recently wrote to me and included a work which deals with the horrors of collecting. It's nice to know that others are in this quandary, too. The poem is called *Collecting: A Modern Paradigm*. The conclusion sends chills through me. It says,

"So, you're either a collector or something collected or both.

And who knows

When we're displaced by our own junk

We might meet at the top of the heap."

I don't know whether I'll succeed, but the next time I pass a closet I'm going to try to throw out all the things in it which I've not used for three or more years. That means more than half the closet. I promise to let you know if I succeed!

I'm not a total disbeliever in ghosts, goblins or mysterious phantoms. In fact, I must confess that there are certain occurrences in my house that defy any rational explanation. For instance, one of the great and perpetual mysteries is where my socks disappear. I can't seem to keep a matching pair. I am continually having to buy new socks. After the first wash, some of them simply vanish.

They never go in pairs, which wouldn't be so bad. The annoying thing is that I am left with one green sock, one blue and one black. I have accumulated a huge pile which I dare not throw out lest a matching sock reappear as mysteriously as it disappeared. So far this hasn't happened.

They certainly can't just walk off. Or can they? I have become slightly neurotic about seeing that socks go into the washer and dryer in pairs, but still they vanish. I've checked the machines for teeth, for escape hatches or mysterious tubes that might eat up or siphon off my socks. This would account for the mystery, but there are no such things in either the washer or the dryer. Check your machine if you don't believe me. I have come to believe that this is just another one of life's frustrations. I still suspect a phantom somewhere in the laundry room just waiting for the rinse cycle to end.

Every bit as strange as the disappearing socks is the mysterious appearance of clothes hangers. I have hundreds in the house and I can't imagine where they come from. I can't ever remember buying a wire clothes hanger, and no matter how many I return to the cleaners, give away or put into the trash, the closets remain full of them. If I had a choice, I'd rather have socks magically appear than hangers.

Speaking of household mysteries, how is it that cookies vanish even when I don't eat them? Especially the chocolate chip-macadamia nut clusters? I fill the cookie jar on the kitchen sink at great expense. (Do you know that at some cookie stores the cookies are now weighed and sold by the ounce?) Within days they're gone!

This is especially true on weekends when they seem to vanish faster than ever. I know it's not me. I steadfastly ration myself to one or two a day. No one else in the house, including the cat, who loves chocolate, will accept the blame. Still, when I crave a cookie most, the cookie monster, or whatever it, he, or she might be, has been there before me.

I've tried giving up cookies, but before long, I go into withdrawal. So I fill up the cookie jar and resign myself to ending up with only a portion of them.

I'm convinced also that certain cooking ingredients go the way of the cookies. As much as I love cooking and creating gourmet dishes, I'm at a loss to explain how just the ingredient I need is always missing. Where has the vanilla gone? The curry? The cumin? The oregano? I buy these things in giant cans and bottles. In fact, an entire kitchen wall is covered with exotic herbs and seasonings— but where is the one I need?

I once believed that I was alone in these mysteries, but the more I risk talking about them the more people admit to having had similar experiences. I have a friend who constantly loses underwear, another who can't keep shampoos in the house, another who never sends anything to be ironed or cleaned and still has enough wire hangers to make mobiles, planters, wall hangings, back scratchers, or hundreds of other exotic things.

I often wonder if the green sock that's disappeared ends up in someone else's wash. And there's something very strange about the fact that my neighbor never runs out of vanilla!

I think that most people would agree that, though a bit eccentric, I am basically a rational man. I can't help but feel that there must be a good explanation for all of these phenomena. It's obvious that I, for one, have not yet found it. So the mysteries continue.

However, I have found that the sock problem has reached epidemic proportions all over the United States. I am not alone. Friends and family, men and women alike, from all over the country, have offered comfort and helpful suggestions.

There were the practical people who suggested that I simply pin, staple or use string to keep socks together. I've even been told of commercially made clips which guaranteed that the socks would come out as they went in, two by two.

Other practical suggestions included going through the sock drawer at periodic intervals to check on mismatched or escaped single socks.

An entrepreneur came up with a sure-fire plan for selling one-of-a-kind socks, or arranging for mismatched socks to be traded on the open market.

An artist suggested that being fearful of mixing colors is a cultural hangup. She encouraged me to wear mismatched socks fearlessly. "The more outrageous the color combinations the better," she said, "like flowers in a garden."

A less daring person solved the problem by purchasing all his socks in the same color. In this way, he assured me, ". . . I'd not solve the mystery, but I would do away with my problem. After all, isn't life just a series of compromises?"

It's surprising how many people wash their socks in a nylon mesh bag like the ones one gets in the produce department of a grocery store. This way, people say, you wash socks apart from everything else, yet keep them together.

A scientist assures me that is has been scientifically proven that socks disappear and coat hangers keep proliferating because socks are the larvae of coat hangers.

A believer in reincarnation offered that those of us who have a sock problem are paying for some heinous crime we committed in some previous life. Perhaps, he suggests, we were foot muggers who purloined footwear to satisfy some fiendish fetish.

In 1975, even Jules Feiffer, the cartoonist, expressed his puzzlement about missing socks. In his cartoon, his pathetic figure gets down to his last two pairs of socks, when his washing machine sends him a message which reads "Quit trifling with the laws of nature and bring the machine more socks!"

Perhaps the most astounding story came from a husband/father who does the family laundry. He was hounded by his family about their missing socks, but to his great frustration was unable to find a solution. One day a disappearing blue sock, another day a materialized green sock. The problem reached its peak when his wife confronted him and in suspicious tones demanded to know about a strange piece of lingerie which had mysteriously appeared in the laundry. It certainly wasn't hers! As the ensuing battle raged and reached a peak, the mystery was solved when their dog casually came into the laundry room bearing a sock from their neighbor's wash!

There is a psychological theory which suggests that we become less frustrated with problems when we learn how common they are. There is a companion theory which states that the more alternatives we have for solving a problem, the less will be the frustration in trying to solve it. I am therefore grateful to my wise and caring friends and family who took the time from their busy and significant schedules to help me. Although the mystery remains, I shall sleep better now, knowing what good company I keep!

I rarely allow things to irritate me anymore, but one thing that always succeeds in doing so is waiting. Time is so precious, I can't imagine how some people can feel totally unconcerned about squandering it for us. Now, if we want to waste our own time, that's up to us. But I object to others thinking their time has more value than mine.

I have a very wonderful friend. In almost every way he's a delight, but I've never known him to arrive anywhere on time. If he arranges an appointment with you for ten o'clock, you can be certain that you'll be hearing from him at ten-thirty with a frantic telephone call letting you know that he's running a bit late. It's doubly annoying when you've struggled to get up early to have breakfast with him, at his enthusiastic suggestion, only to sit around for an hour awaiting his convenience.

I fully believe that annoyances should be verbalized immediately before they grow into monsters that threaten loving relationships. I have spoken to my friend repeatedly about his lateness. Each time he has a perfectly legitimate excuse: his car wouldn't start; he didn't get his wakeup call; he was winding up a most important meeting with a client; his telephone lines failed. I have no reason to doubt him—perhaps he is prone to catastrophes. But I begin to question all these things happening so consistently. It always upsets me that this man has caused me to waste so many precious hours of my life when I could have been active and productive. This never seems to have occurred to him.

Of course I could decline his invitations. That would certainly stop the problem. But he's such a stimulating, generous and amusing person (when he's there), I would hate losing him as a friend.

I have this same problem with doctors. My appointment is for 1 P.M. I miss lunch to get to his office on time through crowded freeway traffic. I arrive a comfortable ten minutes early and am informed casually that the doctor is running a bit late. I am asked to take a seat and told that he'll be with me as soon as possible. One hour later I am ushered into a small visiting room and again made to wait, this time in a state of uncomfortable undress for another fifteen minutes. The doctor finally appears without so much as an apology and asks, "Well, now, how are we doing today?" It's no surprise that he finds my blood pressure elevated!

I always seem to be the person who arrives on time to meetings, dinner parties, or whatever. I am also always the one who must sit and wait while the others straggle in.

So many people are casual about time that I'm beginning to think I must be the neurotic one. They tell me that being punctual is a sign of obsessive-compulsive tendencies. But I can't feel good about being late. It seems to me to be very presumptuous of those who think that their time has more value than another's.

Naturally there are occasions when it is truly impossible to be punctual. We're caught in an emergency, tied up in traffic, or a myriad of other situations. But for me, it becomes pathological when it happens with almost predictable consistency.

I know that there are many like myself who can identify with the problem. Perhaps we should join forces and simply refuse to wait, or take off on our own after a considerate fifteen minutes of waiting.

The Swiss are among the most punctual people in the world. Perhaps it is because they learn from childhood that trains arrive and leave as scheduled, theater curtains rise as indicated in the program and no one is admitted late, and stores close at their appointed hour. Maybe that is why people without a time sense are so often upset when dealing with Swiss society, and those of us who care about time are so delighted and relieved to be there.

Time waits for no one. I wonder if the day will ever come when we'll be brave enough to do the same.

A
Passion
for
Giving

The great Chinese philosopher Lao Tzu wrote that "Kindness in words creates confidence, kindness in thinking creates profoundness, and kindness in giving creates love."

I've witnessed this scene in restaurants many times. Two men prepare to leave and one grabs for the check. The other attempts to snatch it away from him and the familiar tug of war commences. Each is determined to make his gesture, even if it means straight-arming the other all the way to the cashier. I know the situation, I know the feeling.

The giving and receiving that is a natural part of any relationship often becomes an epic struggle of "whose turn is it now?" Certainly no one wants to be perpetually on the receiving or giving end, but when two people give freely there shouldn't be any need to keep score. That's true whether the giving comes from the pocketbook or the heart.

Children are most often associated with a perpetual "give me" attitude and we tend to be more tolerant of it because they are children. We sometimes forget that they also love to give—a drawing, a favorite rock, a clay impression. Remember what a joyful discovery it was when we first learned that we could make others happy by giving. It was a joy that never grew old. Still, there was always a temptation to equate giving with buying, which was a notion not easily discounted in a society that is so *thing* oriented. With so many occasions for gift giving, we can easily attach more importance to the gift than to the occasion for which it is given.

One of my students told me of a different tradition that is shared by her family. Rather than exchange gifts every 25th of December, they do it at random times throughout the year. Instead of the hectic seasonal shopping experience, each family member waits for the right gift to come along and then gives it as a Christmas present even if it's in June.

If that all sounds like it's not in keeping with the spirit of things, quite the contrary was true in this family. We

119

should be reminded every Christmas that presents are but a token symbol of a far more significant gift. This spirit should be with us the year round. My student felt that the traditional day was made more wondrous, less commercial, and the focus was more highly spiritual. Their way, the spirit of Christmas extends throughout the year and it becomes something they want to do instead of something dictated by custom.

But the spirit of giving comes in many forms, and in this country there's certainly no shortage of selfless contributions of time, money and caring wherever it is needed. Last year over 40 million people worked an average of nine hours a week as volunteers in hospitals, schools, convalescent homes, health agencies, international relief organizations, etc. So often statistics are misleading, but in this case there is a positive commitment to give where it is needed and where only tangible rewards are offered.

Receiving is another part of giving and it's not always the easiest thing to do with grace. A friend of mine is thrown into a dither every Christmas, mailing out cards as she receives them from others. Getting an unexpected present without reciprocating is a particular horror for her to contemplate. Everything must be entered in a ledger and a balance must be struck for her own piece of mind. It seems that she came from a family where very meticulous attention was always given to equality in all things. Giving to one meant having to give to all. What was no doubt intended to be a system of fairness probably ended in promoting more pettiness and jealousy than anything else.

One who gives in love, whether it is a dazzling present or a thoughtful compliment, is always repaid when it is received in the same spirit. Just as listening is at least half of the art of communicating, the art of receiving with joy, appreciation and sensitivity is every bit as important as the giving.

• • •

Sometimes we need to be reminded just how important it is that we participate in the welfare and growth of others. It's all too easy to fold our arms and ask, "What can I do?," or make the all-too-familiar statement, "Sorry, no time." For many, this can become a way of life.

When I was teaching in the public schools, I can remember the many teachers' meetings and seminars we were obliged to attend. The purported purpose was to come together in order to focus more clearly on the main goals of education. Always, no matter how we worded our objectives or devised our formulas, the one recurring theme year after year was the need for total involvement. From the policymakers to the implementers and the recipient students, the key ingredient in a successful education program was the active participation of everyone.

Anyone who has ever studied successful business practices knows that one of the main requirements is that of working together, from the administrative level to each worker. Where this is accomplished, the result is invariably a successful business with high achievement and production levels. There is a definite correlation.

I remember a retired doctor who came to one of the schools where I taught. He told the principal that he lived nearby and that he wanted to volunteer his services in whatever capacity he was needed. He wanted to help out in the classroom. He had no relatives in attendance or any vested interest in making the offer. He simply wanted to help, as an aide or a tutor, to share some of his knowledge and experience. In retirement he finally had plenty of time and had chosen this place and this time to extend himself. He was determined to continue to be a positive force in the lives of others.

Naturally, the principal and the teaching staff were a little overwhelmed. That sort of thing doesn't happen very much, not anywhere. The doctor soon became invaluable. He gave much. His specialties were health education and math, but more important than what he contributed to those subjects was his example to the children. They loved him. His warm presence and desire to become involved was a beautiful object lesson in human relations: to give of oneself without expecting anything in return is one of the finest things one human being can do for another.

Stories such as this inevitably bring on the skeptics. After all, there must be an angle. We are constantly told that nothing is free, that every investment must have a return. Certainly our doctor friend was greatly rewarded for his selfless involvement with those children, but in intangible ways. Whether or not we care to admit it, he was a model for the kind of people we most need and appreciate.

Even if we are suspicious of anyone who would give of himself to strangers, we can perhaps give some thought to our commitments closer to home. In my neighborhood there is a daycare center which I pass every day. I see young children waiting, often into the evening, for a parent to reclaim them. Once having done that, I sometimes imagine that it's a quick dinner, a little time in front of the television set, then off to bed, ready to be packed off the next day.

I don't mean that to sound like an indictment of the many families who find it necessary to participate in such a routine. For better or worse, having two parents working is a present reality for many children. Whether by choice or economic necessity, the result is less involvement within the family.

This means that a more concentrated effort is required in seeing that the time they do have together is of the highest quality. They will have to try to be more intuitive in deciding when to stop everything and take time to listen, or give support, or just be there to love.

Each of us sooner or later realizes that our relationships with others require giving of ourselves—not only of our time, but our sincere and caring involvement as well. Too often we close the book on the many who need us by allotting just so much of ourselves, and end by being miserly with what should be the easiest and least expensive thing to give—ourselves.

It was years ago when I first saw Hong Kong. I was told that it was the Jewel of the Orient. It's true. I was enthralled by its beauty. The vista from Victoria Peak is awesome, no matter the nature of the weather or the time of day. It's so peaceful there, high above the city, and strangely quiet, considering the explosion of activity that is just below. But I also loved the hustle and bustle of humanity around the Star Ferry, which connects the Kowloon part of the city with the Hong Kong side. Throngs of people pack the ferry boats at every hour.

I loved sitting there under a lamplight at dusk, watching on one side the changing colors of the harbor and on the other the rush of hundreds of commuters going home.

On one such evening, I noticed a very young man who sat not too far from me on the same bench. He was engrossed in a book and seemed oblivious to the noisy passengers and the deepening sunset. In the week that followed I discovered that no matter how frequently I went to my bench in the evening the same studious young man was always there.

One night he turned to me and queried, in very halting English, "Could you help me to say this word?" I found that the book which had so entranced him was an English-Chinese dictionary. After I had helped him with the word, he told me that his name was Wong and that he was trying to teach himself English. He did this so he could get a good job and make a better life for himself and his large family.

Wong and I became fast friends. We met almost nightly after that at the Star Ferry. He became my tour guide and helped me to find my way around Hong Kong. I became his English conversation teacher.

Wong's story was a poignant one. He and his family, though proud and willing to work, were existing at a level just above desperation. Wong was the eldest son of a family of eleven, and the only one working. Armed only with a dictionary, his prospects for a better life seemed a distant dream. Though I was traveling on a very limited budget, I decided that I could help. Before leaving Hong Kong, I arranged for his tuition at an English language school.

I was gone from the United States for a little over two years. When I returned there was a note from Wong. He was on his way to mastery of English. He had found a new, better-paying job and was able to raise the standard of living for everyone in his family. Enclosed in his letter was a bank note for a few dollars to repay what he saw as his debt to me.

I returned the money with a note which read something like this: "Wong, please take the money down to the Star Ferry and when you find a young man sitting there under a street lamp, trying to learn English from a dictionary, give him the money from both of us, with love." Wong got the message. I can only hope that he passed it along, and that each one touched will have touched another.

For longer than we can remember we've been reminded that love isn't love until it's given away. All over the world I've found this expressed with more and more frequency. Despite language barriers, I discovered that an expression of true love could never be misinterpreted. There were many who shared their food even though it was in meager supply. There were individuals who went miles out of their way to escort me to my destination, concerned about my getting lost. There were strangers who shared their lives, with touching vulnerability. These were all expressions of love given freely.

Though individually we may not be capable of affecting world peace and understanding, it is a cause served by each single act of love and kindness, whenever and wherever they happen. One of our best hopes continues to lie in the individual—the small acts of kindness we can each perform, the infectious cheer we can spread, the generous act we can perform without expectation of reward, the show of tenderness, the moment of nurturing, the time given in support.

Recently I received a letter from a reader who wrote, "You are always so positive about life, so hopeful about loving and about people's behavior that it was an inspiration for me to get out of myself a bit more. I wanted to explore the art of giving which you so often encourage. I'm rather young and don't have much to give, so I decided to buy a bunch of daisies, stand at a local intersection, and hand them out with a simple, 'Have a beautiful day.' I thought it would be fun and might help to make others a bit happier. It ended by being a very enlightening experience—not exactly what I expected, but I learned a lot about human nature.

"It surprised me how few people would accept my gift. Many just passed me by, avoiding my smile. Others actually pushed my hand away. Some simply uttered a curt 'No thank you' and moved on their way. Others reluctantly took the flower and waited for some pitch, wondering what they had to give in return. The saddest thing I learned was that people are suspicious of giving. It's as if they're afraid that taking will commit them in some way. I wasn't even able to get rid of all my daisies. I went home with some of them drooping in my hand. What a strange world this is!"

It's unfortunate but nonetheless true that we live in a world of skeptics. Some individuals are constantly on their guard, unwilling to accept the possibility that there may be an honest person around, or that acts of kindness and goodness happen all the time. In a real sense, we're all responsible for this attitude and in small ways perpetuate it. We are products of our experiences. If someone has offered us a rose and immediately followed up with a plea for a donation, we naturally form a mindset against such future occurrences. From that time on, every rose offered may be suspect.

There are few of us who are without some experience which has left us disillusioned and feeling duped. We are pounced upon at airports and supermarkets by people offering all kinds of things in seemingly good faith, only to be followed by a plea for donations or support for some special cause. We are sent free samples of products, supposedly only in the spirit of good public relations and our valued opinions, but later find that we've been coerced into buying something out of a feeling of obligation.

This sort of behavior can even be seen between lovers. We are convinced of another's love, only to find later that it has been given with expectations and conditions. It is natural, then, that we become a little more doubtful, a little less receptive. In a society where one doesn't often encounter selflessness and real generosity, it's not surprising that we build defenses against them.

I have a good friend who loves to participate in swap meets. Once he created a small area in his booth where he placed objects marked "free"—things he simply wanted to give away. He was surprised to find that no one took them. Finally, he attached a low price to each of the items and they quickly disappeared, leaving him a few dollars richer, but a great deal more confused about human behavior. This was another example of people's conviction that "everything has its price," that "nothing's free in this world."

It seems to me that there is an important lesson to be learned from all this. If we enjoy giving and see what a desperate need our world has for it, if we want to disprove the skeptics, we must be willing to take a few rejections and be tolerant of eccentric behavior. Giving without expectations is a very positive action, which must not be extinguished because of occasional negative and thankless responses.

My suggestion to the young girl was that she continue to offer her flowers if that is her way of expressing herself and it gives her pleasure. Perhaps others will eventually see that she is indeed sincere. They will then be richer—if not with a total change in attitude, at least by a flower given freely in the spirit of love.

According to a recent Gallup Poll, 55 percent of Americans are volunteers who contribute their time to improving society. This is a very interesting statistic. I've heard that people have a tendency to shade the truth in polls. We like to think of ourselves as being actively engaged in helping others, so who's going to feel comfortable responding to this poll negatively?

Helping others is one of the most rewarding experiences we can share. In fact, it is usually the helper who is helped through helping! Studies show that owning pets or plants promotes a longer and healthier life simply because they require the owner's helping hand. It gives meaning to existence—something to get out of bed for.

We come from a long tradition of helping each other. Americans were brought up on barn raisings, bucket brigades, quilting bees and cake sales. We are known for our positive and immediate response to those in need. Our telethons and fund-raisers bring in thousands of dollars for Olympic teams, the physically impaired and hunger victims in many parts of the world. The problem, however, is that these causes are one-shot deals—we give, then forget. Somehow we lose sight of the fact that need is ongoing. It's all too easy to sit back and say, "I've done my bit," as if giving is done in quotas.

There are many deterrents to giving. Some say they don't know how to help or where to direct their services. We don't have to *know* how—we can be taught. And we don't have to *know* where—we just need to look about us.

We say that we don't have time. This is perhaps the weakest of all excuses. The greatest expenditure of free time in the United States is spent watching television. The average is about six hours a day, and that produces little more than boredom, passivity and extra fat where it isn't wanted. If each of us were to surrender just one night a week, there would be millions of free hours to give others.

We sometimes take a narrow view of what it means to give. We associate giving with money. Of course money is important, but there is no amount that can buy the value of someone who will sit with a dying person who would otherwise be alone. Or someone who will deliver a warm meal to an elderly house bound individual, or volunteer to teach reading, or just listen to a person who is afraid, lonely or rejected.

I recently boarded a flight to New York. The stewardess shouted with delight when I entered the plane. "I've wanted to meet you for such a long time. May I talk with you later?" she asked. When she got a break, she sat next to me and frantically told her story—a cheating husband, a disturbed child, a feeling of despondency and helplessness, a fear of being unable to cope. After a long while she stopped in midsentence and sighed deeply with relief. She wiped her tears and sat up in the seat. "Oh, Dr. Buscaglia," she said, "you've helped me so much." I hadn't said a word. Sometimes helping can mean just listening, without judgment or advice.

We never become more visible or meaningful than when we help someone else. What we do, after all, is a tangible statement about who we are, what we value and how we feel about ourselves and our world. Author Helen Colton says the way to find what we can best do is to ask ourselves what we love or hate with a passion and then do something about it.

The world is in great need of helpers. We who inhabit it cannot survive without them. Our growth and our survival depend upon our willingness to give to each other. It's a well-worn adage, but nonetheless true, that "love isn't love until it is given away." Until it's manifested through some caring act, love is nothing more than a very good idea—only an idea, a simple word, a notion in the abstract.

There is something for each of us to do. We become truly human at the moment when we reach out to help someone.

A
Passion
for
Growth
and
Acceptance

I agree that there is perhaps no greater joy in life than to find ways of overcoming our weaknesses. We know all about the thrill of victory and the agony of defeat. We seem to encounter obstacle after obstacle. Still, with hope, dignity, a little madness, and some belief in the self, we can make great strides toward achieving our goals. The greatest failure is to fail to try. Many of us have probably given up just when, with a bit more persistence and patience, we would have made it. So often when all seems lost everything points to failure, then comes the breakthrough.

Loneliness is fast becoming the great American malaise. It seems to ignore age, gender and socioeconomic levels. Surveys tell us that one quarter of the population suffers from chronic loneliness. It is among the leading causes of suicide. Books and magazines are consistently full of information and advice for the lonely—be more aggressive, step out and meet people, you have a right to be you, get out of that shell of your own making, celebrate life, count your blessings. Though sometimes good advice, these remedies seem to be of small comfort to the lonely.

No one need be told that loneliness can be very painful. In fact, it can cause us to feel almost totally devastated. It produces counter-productive feelings, discourages risk and saps emotional resources. It is not surprising that people will even elect to remain in completely unfulfilling relationships rather than risk being alone.

We all know that loneliness has little or nothing to do with being physically alone. In fact, some of the most lonely among us are constantly in crowds, surrounded by people. No matter what our situation, most of us will at one time or another experience loneliness.

Few of us prepare ourselves for these possibilities. We carefully save our money for the future, we insure ourselves against economic reverses and prepare for countless unpredictable occurrences, but we do little about the time when we may have to face things alone, or find ourselves disconnected from others.

I have hundreds of letters from such individuals. They tell me they have suddenly been forced through loneliness to struggle with feelings of emptiness and unworthiness. They discover themselves on their own—some for the first time in their lives—and have no resources to call upon to contend with it. They seem to find little inner reserve or strength, or more important, no real sense of self.

It has been found that what people do in such a situation depends more upon how they feel about themselves than any other single factor. It is not so much a matter of fighting loneliness as it is using the strength that comes from self-knowledge to put it into its proper perspective.

Loneliness is never pleasant. It will always require us to actively work through a period of adjustment or healing. But this time can also to be one of learning and growth, for it compels us to examine and reevaluate ourselves and the world we've created, to get to know ourselves better.

It is a pity that we often wait until loneliness is strangling us before we try to understand its complexities. Still it's understandable, since we are brought up to avoid being alone, as if it were some type of antisocial behavior. Our young lives are often spent filled with planned social activities and interactions. We are encouraged to join clubs, teams, classes. We often become so busy that to find ourselves alone, faced with some nonscheduled time, is to many an almost devastating experience.

Heaven forbid that we should have an unplanned weekend! No one tells us that it's perfectly normal to want to be alone, to have private times when we can tune in to our own needs and desires, guided only by our own resources, or carried away by our spur of the moment impulses and dreams. We all need our separate worlds, apart from others, where we can quietly retire for regrouping, for getting back in touch with ourselves. We need this personal solitary place as a pleasant alternative to our more public lives. We must treasure this part of our existence as much as we do the more social part. Then, when loneliness comes, we will have that special place to fall back upon.

It is wonderful to have significant and loving people in our lives. We cannot live in complete happiness without them. But we must not allow ouselves to depend so completely upon them that we lose our sense of separateness.

There should always be an inner place we can count on that is solely ours.

To conquer loneliness we shall each have to assume the sacred responsibility of becoming a complete person. And most of all, to define ourselves without always including someone else in the definition.

The brochure we receive in the mail is all about victims. Along with a frightening picture of a battered woman is a very calculated message that it's high time we realize that we're all potential victims of violence. The brochure does not calm our fears, rather it capitalizes on them—we had better insure ourselves against possible crime. The statistics this ad cites are indeed alarming: a crime is committed every two seconds in the United States; in the past five years the number of violent crimes has increased more than twenty percent; nearly one-third of all households will be victimized by violence at some time.

How easily we can become intimidated not only by such statistics, but by the vague feeling of impending disaster that they create in our minds. More disturbing is the fact that we can become victims of our own fears, and fear can dominate our very lives. What statistics tell us is often what the researcher or advertiser interprets. For example, the chances of being killed in an auto accident is nearly ten times greater than being the victim of a violent crime. It can happen just as suddenly and just as brutally, yet how many of us cower in our homes afraid to drive?

There is unquestionably too much violence in America. No one doubts that each tragic instance is deserving of our strongest condemnation. But when it causes us to retreat in any way from full enjoyment of life, it is time to bring such fears into perspective.

Consider just a few examples of how quickly and completely we are seized by fear:

After several episodes of sabotaged candy given out at Halloween in recent years, many children throughout the country have been kept indoors on that very special night. There is even a growing sentiment that we phase out the holiday in order that we may protect our children.

A box of Girl Scout cookies was found to have a straight pin wedged in one of its cookies. On the same day, every local T.V. station headlined this newest danger to our children's well-being. X-ray centers were even set up for any who were fearful of biting into their cookies. Isn't it amazing how readily we sensationalize the demented schemes of a few twisted individuals and how they can dominate our lives?

Increasingly I hear of parents who live in constant fear that some calamity will befall their children. One young mother I talked to would not allow her children to play in front of their home, let alone go to the playground, for fear that they would be kidnapped. One cannot guarantee her that such a thing will never happen any more than she can be assured that a plane will never crash into her house. If we choose to live our lives fully, we must be willing to encounter risks along the way. One necessarily involves the other.

Fears and anxieties also have an unfortunate way of putting masks on people. Strangers are viewed for the potential harm they may cause instead of the growth and joy they might offer. Trust gives way to suspicion. Caring involvement with others is replaced by watching out for number one.

We are told repeatedly that one of the greatest deterrents to crime is a sense of community, of neighborliness, even of watchful concern for one another. I remember an old gentleman who lived on the street where I grew up. He was, as far as the block was concerned, a one-man Neighborhood Watch. With the least activity anywhere on the street, he was reliably present at one of his windows, peering through his curtains. We regarded him as something of a busybody, but at the same time were comforted by his vigilance. Nothing escaped his watchful eye.

I'm not suggesting that we all become sentries and watchdogs. Instead, we might consider coming out of our houses a little more often, if for no other reason than to feel more connected to our neighbors. Sometimes our fears are magnified simply because we feel alone in facing them. While the inner sanctums of our homes do provide a sort of insulation from the world, they can also isolate us from it. Surely our streets and neighborhoods can become more hospitable places when we are more together with the people in them.

How much more manageable our fears become when we learn to expand our definition of family and recognize that we're all in this together. We need each other. Fear is said to be the primary disease of the twentieth century. As we approach the end of this hundred years, perhaps we will come to learn that a caring involvement for each other might be a cure.

I don't imagine there is anyone fully alive who has not felt discouraged. The word *discourage* is defined as to deprive of courage, hope or confidence. Phrases such as, "It's not worth it," "I can't," "I give up," "I've failed," are standard. None of us is a complete stranger to feelings of hopelessness. It is usually because we feel disappointed or trapped or have lost our sense of direction and hope for the future.

Discouragement is a very human attribute. We need not censure ourselves for feeling it. But it is important to know that no matter what the circumstances that have brought us to this point, they are not insurmountable. The world is full of possibilities; and, as long as there are possibilities, there is hope. Even the most successful and happiest people can tell you about having spent time questioning themselves, their values and their abilities. But they have never lost the capacity to hope.

There is a man whom we all know. His history goes as follows: Twice he failed in business. He ran for the state legislature and for Congress twice and failed. He was defeated twice in Senate races. He worked hard to become Vice President of the United States with no success. The woman he loved died when she was very young. Eventually he suffered a nervous breakdown. Through all of this he had the self-knowledge and strength to overcome adversity, continue with life and become President. His name, of course, is Abraham Lincoln.

We are inspired by such a message. But we are not all Lincolns. Still, there is much to be learned by his example and the examples of other survivors. Because something goes wrong does not mean that it's the end of the world. In fact, it may be the challenge we need to awaken us to our strengths. The real dilemma is the feeling that there is no way to turn, no place to go, no one to help us. What is important to remember is that there are many solutions to every problem. We are not perfect and may make mistakes but all things come to an end. Armed with this knowledge we are halfway to a solution.

There were many times when I was growing up that could have been devastating for the entire family. Times when Papa had lost his job, when there was no money even for the bare necessities, when things truly looked hopeless. In spite of, or perhaps especially because of, those times, Mama and Papa never allowed us to lose our sense of humor, sense of self, or the assurance that we'd find a way. Somehow, we always did.

I was fortunate to have learned this early in life. I know that after experiencing discouragement, the first thing I try to do is keep in mind that nothing lasts forever, that only I can decide what I can do to make things better. With this hope and faith in the future I'm off and running, again seeking new solutions.

I believe that the truly healthy person is the one who has the greatest number of alternatives for any behavior. We are limited only by our willingness to discover these alternatives. Let's say that we find ourselves in tears. There is nothing wrong with tears. They often sharpen our ability to see. We then need to ask ourselves if crying forever is what we want to do. If not, we must consider what else we can possibly do to help ourselves and solve our problem.

We can consider possible alternatives. It may be helpful to find what others have done in similar situations. With a list of alternatives in hand, we will feel less trapped and more in a position to decide what is best for us.

Finally comes the greatest step: We must *do* something. In action comes true knowledge and a wonderful sense of freedom. We are never really trapped. Discouragement at times seems inescapable. But, to remain in this state is a waste of time, energy and life. We can learn to put discouragement aside. When we do, we can get on with life.

There is a park near my home where I used to jog every evening. These days it invites me to take a brisk walk. In slowing down I've become more attuned to the surroundings that I was pounding and panting my way through before.

A few months ago, I noticed more and more parents practicing baseball in the park with their children. One youngster told me that tryouts for Little League were approaching and, "You gotta be good if you wanna make the team." Little League being the institution that it is, I understand the anticipation that goes along with "making the team."

Once in a while I'll see a father and son throwing and catching and batting long after the sun has set. The father is patient with his son's clumsiness, yet he also seems determined to make a ballplayer of him. The son wants to please Dad, but it's painfully obvious, in some cases, that baseball may not be the way. Given a choice, he may wish he were home with his chemistry set or exploring the woods—anything but this struggle with bat and ball and glove.

Most of us have seen this drama played out before. Certainly some of these youngsters will learn the game and gain much from the experience, but I'd guess that some will also feel frustration. Their talents may lie elsewhere and, therefore, go unnoticed.

Each of us possesses gifts that make us distinct. These qualities only await recognition and development. The problem is they may not always be what others expect. For instance, Eddie is sitting on the end of the bench waiting to get into the game. He can't hit a ball, but he has marvelous musical talent. And there, buried in the third row of dancers, is Beth, stomping her way through her tenth ballet recital. She'd rather be learning about animals, a subject that has interested her for a long time.

Eric is a stargazer. Like Einstein, who hated formal schooling, he dreams of distant corners of the universe and faraway planets. His teachers say he is inattentive and a daydreamer. His parents don't understand why his grades are poor. One day he is given a telescope and a new world opens up to him. Now the universe is limitless. Perhaps his future is better focused.

I remember a student (I'll call him Rodney) who was classified as a below-average student. He had behavioral problems and a poor academic performance. Nothing we did seemed to have any effect on him. He was continually late to class and always had an unusual excuse: A sparrow had fallen to the ground and needed to be returned to its nest; a five-car accident happened in front of his house and he had to get the ambulance. All sorts of calamities and strange occurrences seemed to delay Rodney, especially on his way to school.

One morning, in desperation, I assigned him a one-page composition in which he was to explain in detail what happened to him that day. He had no trouble writing several pages. In fact it was an unusually fascinating piece of fiction. It was easy to see Rodney's uniqueness—he was a born storyteller. Before the year was over, Rodney was turning out tales about all sorts of things. He became interested in ideas and was inspired by other authors. He read avidly and was far more interested in his education. He even started coming to school on time.

Our educational system often fails to identify individual talents that make each student unique. Instead we place greater emphasis on long-term, specific objectives and standards that must be met by all. This often creates the boredom and apathy that causes spark and creativity to wane and die.

We hear from time to time about some individuals who have conquered the system. There is no doubt that when this occurs everyone benefits, for it is from this that art is created, mystery understood and dreams are made real.

• • •

It is interesting how often we look back at our past with fondness. We talk about the good old days when life seemed less complicated and more carefree. (Was there ever really a time that was not complicated?) It may be that complex images of our past simply become glossed over by time and memory. But the most significant aspect about this yearning is our deep desire to uncomplicate our lives. It isn't that we're asking to retreat to some rural outpost and spend the remainder of our days in quiet meditation and communion with nature. It simply means that most of us seem overburdened with responsibilities, worry, and a belief in a continual need to strive for more.

However, I believe that most of us would go mad if we had to give up much of our complicated life patterns. I have a friend, for instance, who sets out each year for a week of camping alone in Yosemite National Park. All year he gives lip service to the importance of this escape for maintaining his continued sanity and physical well-being. When the appointed time comes, he leaves his wife and children; and, with tent, canteen, hiking boots, air mattress and sleeping bag in tow, sets off for the valley and his much sought-after solitude. It never fails that he returns after only a few days, having had his fill of peace and quiet.

We sometimes hear affluent people recall the early days of their relationships when they had little of monetary value, a small one-room apartment, an old car and a slim bank balance. Yet they refer to those days as among the happiest they have ever known. Still, as we mature, we don't seem to strive for the simple lives we claim to want. In fact, we work to increase our gains because we never seem to have enough.

We fail to recognize that the more we own, the more we are possessed by what we own—that more is not necessarily better. In time we even begin to define ourselves by the number of things we possess. Perhaps it is well to remember that the only things we can take with us are those which will fit into a coffin.

Prior to their marriage, two former students of mine learned the value of simplicity. They nearly broke their engagement over the trials of planning the ceremony. The printer, the caterer, the florist, the dresses, the tuxedos, the rental agencies, the reception hall, the band and you mustn't forget the monogrammed matchbooks!

Then there was the guest list with each side questioning the other and worrying about who might be offended. And the registration of china, crystal and silverware patterns, and bath towels and linens, ad infinitum. The staggering number of decisions, the frayed nerves, the frantic anticipation were almost too much. Here were two people very much in love. The only wish they had was to declare their love in a formal way before friends and family. They had looked forward to their special day all of their young lives but were barely on speaking terms before the ceremony.

On the other hand, I recently watched a little girl flying a kite in the park below my house. There she was with a few sticks, paper, string, a little wind and a great expanse of sky—the simplest of activities. She didn't have to go far from home. She was totally caught up in the moment, mesmerized by the gentle movements of the kite. She stayed in the park for a long while, totally at peace.

Really, life is simple. It is we who are complex. Of course, when I say this I am challenged with the naiveté of such a statement. The retort I most often hear is "Well, that may be true of your life, but there's nothing simple about mine!" I am tempted to say that if life is not simple, we may be responsible for its complexities. And if we desire it to be otherwise, it's never too late.

Of course we should strive to become all that we can and do all that is possible to make the world a better place

in which to grow in joy. We should strive to obtain those
things which we feel we need to make our lives more comfortable and satisfying. But we must never allow those
things to dominate.

When the clutter, anxiety and complications threaten
to hem us in, we should bring to mind the words of Thoreau, "Simplify! Simplify!" And if even this fails, we might
learn from the children and go fly a kite!

Everyone is out there these days finding themselves.
No one is left minding the store. It's a growing epidemic.
Never in our history have so many people become obsessed with the need to know themselves, and never in
our history have so many become lost, confused and de-
spairing in the process.

Happily, the past three decades have been times of
changing attitudes, values and roles. We are finally able
to admit (some still reluctantly) that women are as wise,
creative and able as men. We have finally been forced to
recognize that they have the right to succeed, grow and
contribute to the extent of their abilities; that for those who
so desire, there must be no limitations placed in the way
of becoming all that they are able to be.

Things are changing for men, too. They are discovering at last how much better it is to have an efficient,
capable and interesting woman around than the somewhat
empty role model of *wife*. Men are finding new joy in sharing full responsibility for the social, economic and psychological climate of their homes and families. They have
found that in sharing tasks, for instance, both husband and
wife are released for more productive, special and personal
time.

These discoveries have forced many to redefine roles,

to decry the loss of so many years and to set out with determination to rectify this by dedicating themselves to the task of seeking their true selves.

I know a couple who were happily married for eleven years. Then the wife took a psychology course in personal growth. Through it she was convinced that she was missing life being *simply* a wife and mother. She learned the jargon about waste of human potential, the value of the individual, the search for identity. Somewhere out there, she decided, was the woman she wanted to be. Before the class ended she left her husband and their four children in the *search for self*.

I'm not condemning her actions. In fact, I was equally as eager in my own search. It led me around the world twice. I left family, friends, a promising career and wandered the mountains of Nepal and Valleys of the Moon. I listened to the great gurus, I read the mystical texts, I joined monasteries and ashrams. I studied yoga and meditation techniques. I admit that there was value in this. A search is always exciting and full of newness. But along the way I found that my search was not bringing me any closer to finding that elusive *me*.

Eventually I returned. I had experienced wonderful things and had made many new and lasting friends. I had acquired a great deal of knowledge, but once home found that there was nothing I had discovered on my trip that I could not have found in my own backyard. Of course, it would not have been so exotic or dramatic, nor would it have made such exciting dinner conversation. But what I had needed to discover—myself—was always with me.

Understanding oneself is a worthy and commendable goal. But it is not necessary to leave everything and everyone in order to do it. My friend's wife, for example, found that singles bars, sexual freedom, loneliness, and mystical teachings afforded her a no more conducive environment to knowing herself than would a sympathetic husband, an understanding family, friends and a secure home.

Change is always difficult. People who feel that they have been denied experiences or made wrong choices and have consequently missed life can become frantic about their sense of loss. Rightfully so. There is no greater loss for all of us than a life unlived. But we should keep in mind, before we leave on a search, that even the philosophies most dedicated to knowing ourselves tell us that self-knowledge and enlightenment can come through making a loaf of bread, growing a beautiful garden, or hearing a piece of music.

Oscar Wilde said that, "Only the shallow know themselves," and he was right. There can be no end to the process of self-discovery if we are continually learning, growing and changing. Knowing oneself is a process, not a goal. No one person or place is more conducive than any other in helping this process along.

The tools are not out there somewhere. They are inside of us. Only we can assume the challenge of our voyage. The experience becomes more valuable and meaningful when we take those we love with us along the way. The search for ourselves takes on real meaning when each day becomes a Bon Voyage party.

Any serious human relationship takes work. Not so much in the sense of learning the right rules or formulas that govern all relationships (if there were such things), but in two individuals working together to find what is best for both of them. How people compromise, for instance, says much about the kind of relationship they've worked out together.

Two very dear friends have been struggling with a

compromise of sorts in their marriage. It all has to do with a motorcycle. The husband has owned one from the beginning of their marriage, much to the displeasure of his wife. She has pleaded all along that he search for a safer way to experience the freedom and exhilaration of the outdoors, as he likes to put it. So he has given in a little bit over the years by riding it only occasionally. She in turn has stopped nagging and only says a quiet little prayer for his safe return each time he goes out on it.

This has worked well for twelve years. Recently, however, he was in a very serious accident from which, miraculously, he emerged unscathed. Nearly realizing her worst fears, his wife revived her campaign, this time insisting that he get rid of the motorcycle once and for all. As she sees it, he has a family and future to think about, and continuing his "Sunday on the road with the wind in my face" shows a lack of responsibility.

He countered, now somewhat less forcefully, that his motorcycle represents freedom for him. On this he was adamant. He was the rock of Gibraltar. He would not move.

Friends and family were brought into the argument. I was present when it was being discussed around a dinner table, and when it appeared that things were heating up a bit, someone suggested that a compromise might be worked out. Surely there was some way to handle this situation to the satisfaction of both parties. After all, they were intelligent adults. All sorts of alternatives were offered. Some were absurd, some were practical, but they had all of us, including the main actors in this little drama, seeing some sign of compromise in the whole thing, providing a ray of hope. It was finally agreed that all future motorcycle riding would be confined to off-road trails where the chance of injury was far less than on city streets. The husband acquiesced to this. The marriage was saved.

I wonder how many of us stake out areas in our relationships where we refuse to budge. "It's a matter of principle," we say. Or sometimes we just fold our arms with an air of finality as if to say, "That's just the way it is." Right or wrong, we take our stand. We put on our granite faces and use phrases such as "over my dead body" or "not until hell freezes over."

Certainly there are some things in life that are not easily compromised. Where serious principles are concerned, we may be less inclined to meet someone halfway. But often we maintain that it is our pride or honor that requires us to hold to a position when actually our own self-interest may be the hidden reason.

I am reminded of a woman who called in to a radio talk show I guest-hosted recently. She had worked herself into quite a state over her husband's near total obsession with watching football. She was particularly distressed by a huge radar dish he had put atop their house to bring into their home virtually every football game telecast in this hemisphere. "He parks himself in front of the television set and watches game after game, day after day, from September through January. When I complain, he tells me I might try to develop a little interest in football." He even offered to take her to a football game.

When I mentioned compromise she was stunned. "I hate football with a passion," she hissed. "Never!" That was that. It sounded like a stalemate that they were just going to have to live with. Still, I'm certain that with some serious, honest communication, just a little movement *toward* instead of away from each other, there would be a solution—and if not a solution, at least a little better understanding.

There is indeed an art to compromising. It's such an important part of any relationship. Perhaps it would do us all some good to consider the "nevers"—all the unequivocal no-way-am-I-going-to-change attitudes that we develop and lock into our personalities. Meeting someone halfway does involve giving in, although too often we hesitate because we look upon it as giving up something. A good compromise is one of the simplest ways to affirm and grow in the love and mutual respect that is so vital to any lasting relationship.

You'd love Peter. He's a real charmer. He speaks with a wonderful Hungarian accent and lives in beautiful comfort high on a hill overlooking his adopted city of Vienna. He is now in his eighties and as alert and challenging as a teenager. He has a most fascinating philosophy. He observes that people seem to live life in three states: the state of *must*, the state of *should*, and the state of *want to*. Happiness according to Peter is determined by how much of our lives is spent in the state of *want to*.

We all know the state of musts. Most of our lives are full of them. They are the many day-to-day necessities of life which must be taken care of whether we like them or not: earning a living, eating, cleaning—tasks which take most of our time.

Don't misunderstand. Peter is not suggesting that these activities are bad. He simply feels that they are *must* things and often fill our lives with dull routine that we'd enjoy being rid of.

Our life also has its share of *shoulds*. These are the things which, unlike eating or sleeping, are not essential for our survival, but are expected of the average person—the little niceties we engage in because we want to be socially accepted. People we visit or have as guests because we feel we should. Cards, thank-you notes, presents we should send. We should take mother to dinner. We should write to our uncle. We should have a dinner party—it's our turn. We would certainly continue to exist without actualizing these shoulds but we pressure ourselves into doing them. They require time, energy, and will.

The third category, according to Peter, is that of *want to*. These are the choice activities of life, those things we are seeing, doing, accomplishing because they amuse us, enhance us and build our sense of self. They vary, of course, with each person. But what they have in common is that they are volitional and result in bringing us joy and fulfillment.

One of the most exciting challenges is to attempt to create a life full of the *want tos*, a life as free as possible from *musts* and *shoulds*. We all can do this if we really want to.

For example, let's say that we are shopping for food, certainly a must for all of us. We detest supermarkets: the crowds, the lines, the carts which keep getting in our way. We anticipate each trip with dread. When we finally get there, we push our cart with determination, rush frantically through the aisles in search of the items we require, and rush out.

In order to change this activity to a *want to*, we might try approaching the market with a new, more open view. We can see it as an adventure, a journey into a blaze of color, texture, odors and design. Oranges, bananas, grapefruit, cherries, tomatoes, lettuce, radishes, leeks, eggplant—all glistening in rows of color and pattern. Canned foods, boxed foods, all in an amazing array of creative packaging. It is easy to see how a trip to the market could be a ticket to a journey into sensual enjoyment. Even the long wait in the checkout line can be made into a pleasant experience. We can try to imagine that each cart we see is an expression of a human personality. The woman with the cart overflowing with steak, ground meat, hot dogs, diapers, gigantic boxes of dry cereals and gallons of milk. What does that tell you! Then there's the man with one lamb chop, one tomato, one frozen dessert and a copy of *Sports Illustrated*. How can these experiences be viewed as *musts?*

As to the *shoulds*, we might try to make shoulds, *why nots?* If that note to your uncle will bring him joy, why not? If the dinner party has the power to please and delight, why not? If it has to be done, why not in joy?

It should be enough to remember that each of us has the power to please, to make the world a better place. Why not?

The greater the number of *want tos*, the more wonderful and happy the life. It certainly is worth a try. Let's start by attempting to drop the words must or should from our language. When we do express them, let's find new ways to make them turn into *want to*. Why not?

A
Passion
for
Life

Life is a dynamic process. It welcomes anyone who takes up the invitation to be an active part of it. What we call the secret of happiness is no more a secret than our willingness to choose life.

As we all know, there are those many very scholarly people who say that the unicorn is a mythical animal and never existed. Many years ago, the Irish Rovers suggested in a song the reason for their disappearance. The song says that unicorns did exist but they were too busy playing and having fun to heed Noah's warning and were drowned in the Great Flood.

Let me begin by saying that I don't buy either explanation. I've seen unicorns—I know they exist. They are sleek, fleet of body and mind, mild-mannered, trusting and easily tamed. I understand that by saying I know unicorns I will be accused of being empty-headed or an undying romantic, and I will admit there is some truth in both accusations. But, you may ask, why risk this and discuss unicorns at all? Because I feel that our world is much in need of them.

They are creatures characterized as unique, mystical, pure in heart and mind, pensive, innocent, trusting, wise, possessing great strength and certain fearlessness when fighting evil. They have also been considered a fragment of divinity. In other words, they represent all of the virtues to which we should aspire as human beings. Unicorns are good, kind, sensitive and loving.

It's so strange that such an incredibly lovely creature has always been an object of the hunt. From the start of recorded history to the twentieth century we have been intrigued with the idea of seeking them out, wounding them, caging them, or worse, killing them. No matter— they refuse to die. Unicorns remain a subject of opera, ballet, poetry, novels and paintings. They appear in the art of every continent and culture, from the scratches on walls of prehistoric caves to the gold-framed paintings on silk-lined corridors of contemporary museums. Hardly anyone visits New York City without making a pilgrimage to the Cloisters to see the glorious tapestries of the "Hunt

155

of the Unicorn." Modern writers such as Günter Grass, W.H. Auden and Tennessee Williams use the unicorn as a symbol to illuminate the problems of our modern world. The spirit of the unicorn refuses to vanish.

Many value the spirit and keep it alive within themselves. They try to be caring, forgiving, trusting, pure of heart, vulnerable and dedicated to the sharing of joy and beauty. These people are often seen as living in the past (the good ol' days) when things were simpler. We are told that in our modern, enlightened society there is no place for unicorns. So when people do encounter them, they are hunted, caged, or killed.

Strange that we always kill our saints. They seem to represent something extremely threatening. They offer a challenge that goodness can exist and it is easier not to have to accept the challenge. We would rather accuse them of being simplistic, naive, unrealistic. We convince ourselves that they are insincere, suspect and phony.

Why is it so difficult for us to express and accept positive human values? When will we stop tormenting our unicorns? It is my feeling that unicorns are not extinct at all—they have simply gone underground. They hide in big cities, quiet forests, deserted beaches and country lanes. Occasionally they come together for a brief time for mutual encouragement, but they soon disperse out of fear of being ambushed.

It is my dream that one day, in the not too distant future, thousands of unicorns will come forward from all over the world, unafraid, to share their warmth, their strength and their love. I know they are to be found, for some days I encounter as many as twenty—in shopping centers, at theatres, on crowded streets. Some days I find only three or four, and I must admit that there are times when not one appears.

Appearing as a unicorn is a great risk. I understand

that. The hunters are still there with bow or gun, ready to kill. But I'd like to remind unicorns that their horns are strong, perhaps stronger than they know. Goodness, beauty and love have survived since the beginning of our time on this earth. A free spirit can never be caged. As Anne Morrow Lindbergh said in her poem about the unicorn, even in captivity it is free.

I am still finding unicorns. I know that they are not extinct. They are to be found almost anywhere. By the way, if you know of any, would you please let me know?

We all have weaknesses. I don't think any of us knows too many perfect people. Actually, I'm not sure I'd want to. Of course, I know people who constantly tell me about overcoming their weaknesses and the joy of approaching the ultimate peace and enlightenment. I'm happy for them, but I have a long way to go. My life is a history of continually dealing with weaknesses and attempting to overcome them. But I've found that life doesn't demand perfection of me—only I do.

For example, I'm a terrible speller. There are times when my secretary can't even guess at the word I've managed to butcher. I recall writing a term paper in high school about the legendary Scheherazade. I titled it "The Tail of Scheherazade." My English teacher commented on the paper in horror, "Really!"

I'm also rotten at sports. I can neither hit nor throw a ball. I was always the bane of my coach's existence, not to speak of my teammates whose groans, each time I went to bat, sounded like the rumbling of Mount Etna.

I have too many weaknesses to list, but the two mentioned always have seemed the most visible. I still can't spell and the older I get the less of a threat I pose to Pete

Rose or Abdul Jabbar. But I've managed to survive. I've managed to write seven books and several articles for professional and popular journals and magazines. It's been great to have editors who do know how to spell. As for sports, I once was a decent jogger and am now a devoted long-distance walker, neither of which has required me to hit or throw a ball.

I've learned to live with these weaknesses happily ever after. In fact, they've taught me humility and how to handle ridicule. And in the process they have rid me of illusions of perfection.

Helen Keller, the great lady who lived her life in deafness and blindness, said, "I thank God for my handicaps, for through them I have found myself, my work, and my God." Certainly this statement is worth pondering as a challenge to us all, each of us having our own handicaps and weaknesses.

Most of my professional life has been spent working with the physically and mentally disabled. I owe much to this experience. These individuals have taught me about will and determination. There were those who were blind who learned to *see* with their fingers and their imaginations. Others were deaf and learned to use circumstances as signals. They used what they had to compensate for what they lacked—strengths to compensate for weaknesses.

All of us have this power. It is a way of achieving a victory over ourselves. Whether we have it naturally or acquire it, it is always there. Some of our weaknesses can be overcome with willingness to learn the necessary skills to do so. Some can't, even when we try. It's impossible for me to understand why I never learned to spell. I'm an avid reader. I enjoy writing. But, oh those words! Still, I get by. I discovered how to use a dictionary. If I couldn't spell the word well enough even to look it up, I learned not to be too proud to ask.

I was not as fortunate with learning to play ball. I was often ignored by teammates and coaches who were far too busy trying to win to take the time to help a loser. Still, with jogging or walking, I can get the exercise I need without the ridicule. I may not win any trophies, but I often get free marathon T shirts!

I was raised on "Try, try again," and discovered that my successes were often in direct proportion to my persistence. "To strive with difficulties and to conquer them is the highest form of human felicity," Samuel Johnson told us. But if we can't overcome some of our weaknesses, all is not lost. As long as we've tried, there was something to be learned in the effort. For example, I've learned a lot and have had a happy life, even if I did give Scheherazade a tail and my gym coaches ulcers.

On February 15, 1984, the world lost a great human being. The wonderful performer Ethel Merman died. Her life was a breathtaking adventure. At 21 she was already a star—a status she never lost. She sang and danced her way through fourteen hit musicals and countless movies. She married four times, suffered the loss of a daughter, and went through surgery to remove a brain tumor. Nothing but death stopped her. She gave life her all until the last. "Always give them the old fire," she was often quoted as saying, "even when you feel like a squashed cake of ice."

The old fire Ethel Merman gave us will be missed. The world is much in need of her vigor and enthusiasm for life. She was a pro as a performer as well as a human being. She kept reminding us throughout her life that anything worth doing is worth doing full speed ahead. Of course, it's not always easy to stay up, especially when you feel more like squashed ice—damp, cold, alone, misunderstood. There is nothing wrong with these feelings, of course. They are a part of life. But there are those who wear them like medals of honor. They can't wait to share their unhappiness, laying their chill upon even the most innocent strangers. They are forever illustrating the old adage, "Misery doesn't only love company, it demands it!"

We all know people whom we love dearly; but as much as we care for them, we always face our encounters with a sense of dread. The moment we ask "How's it going?" they start with a deluge of horrors: Their bursitis is acting up again, they're being abused by their neighbors, nobody really cares about them, they're not long for this world, they think they have cancer, their dear friend Sally is dying, and so it goes. Then they ask why we don't see them more often!

I don't know if Ethel Merman had bursitis or was abused by neighbors, but whatever she was feeling on the evenings I saw her perform, I always left the theater a lot happier, much stronger, and a great deal more positive because of being in her space.

We all enjoy being around enthusiastic people. They have a way of avoiding the usual automatic stimulus-response pattern and create their own script as they go along. It isn't that these individuals are more problem-free than we. I saw Ethel Merman in *Gypsy* three times over a span of a year. Each time her performance was almost too big for the limitations of the theater, but there was always a subtle difference, too. Each audience had unique expectations, responses and reactions. Ethel always played the moment, recognizing the audience's needs and satisfying them, despite her personal feelings at the time. She always acted as if she was there for our pleasure, that this was her first and most important performance. Though doing seven shows a week surely must get tiresome, I never saw a bored Ethel. Like all of us, she must have had times of illness, times of loneliness, even times of despair, but I never saw her down. You might say, "Sure, that's true, but that's her job," and you'd be right. But it tells us that staying up is something of a choice. The great thing about a positive approach to life, a desire to show our best self, is that it produces wonderful side effects. It not only creates a happy space for those in our presence, it encourages others to be more positive themselves.

I recall as a freshman in college perceiving myself as a budding poet. I have since abandoned this vision, much to the relief of the literary community, as well as, and more specifically, my English professor. I was especially proud of a phrase I wrote that poses no threat to T.S. Eliot or c.e. cummings, but it said something for me and still does: "I quietly live my Autumn and joyfully share my Spring." Granted this thought may be appalling to the existentialists and those who demand one hundred percent authenticity all the time, but it has made a great difference in my life, and also, I think, in the lives of those around me.

Personally, I want to thank Ms. Merman (and all the Ethels with fire) for bringing Spring to a world too often in the throes of Winter.

I just finished reading a fascinating history of Alcatraz Island entitled *The Rock*. It is written by Pierre Odier, a California high school teacher. Along with a group of his students he spent a week on that island to learn something of its past and to bring into focus a subject that has been, from the beginning, shrouded in mystery.

He describes quite vividly their experiences in poring

over the completely deserted prison facility, sifting through what evidence remained of human beings who existed in the starkest of conditions. Imagine being in this place of ultimate confinement where all human contact, among inmates, including speaking, was forbidden, all communication with the outside world was virtually nonexistent.

Odier writes that even in the midst of this hellish place there survived some very noble examples of the human spirit: prisoners who devised an entire language of hand signals for conversing, debating, even for carrying on chess games; a guard who risked his job by secretly slipping candy bars to the prisoners on a regular basis—incognito. No one, including the prisoners, ever discovered the identity of that caring individual. Another unidentified guard dressed up as Santa Claus one Christmas to bring some little joy to a place otherwise filled with hopelessness and despair.

The human spirit! As long as we have inhabited the earth, we humans have taken immeasurable pride in our nobler instincts. No matter how often people or societies have attempted to put them down, they rise again—in concentration camps, in prisons such as Alcatraz, and in many places where one would expect to find precious little evidence of this spirit.

Recently a documentary was done on California farmworkers. They were asked where they got the strength to return to the fields day after day in an endless struggle for survival. Their answers revealed individuals determined to maintain dignity and purpose in their lives: "We are accustomed to the soil and have faith in God." "I work with my thoughts constantly on my children and a better future." "We have learned to do our jobs well and in that we gain satisfaction."

These are people who work long, hard hours. Their

tasks are back-breaking and very repetitive. Their rewards are meager. Yet in spite of this, there persists a spirit of dedication, not to some higher work authority, but to their own self-respect as human beings.

All of us were schooled in the tradition of learning admirable traits by studying inspiring examples of courage and persistence. When we did this we found that as long as there has been war, there have also been peacemakers; as long as we have been plagued with disease, there have also been healers. As long as there was pain and confusion, there were scientists and other researchers laboring to find solutions; and as long as there was ignorance in the world, there were always willing teachers to help guide us toward greater enlightenment.

These examples taught us to have courage in facing our own obstacles by learning that the human spirit has the power to rise above all odds. We discovered that we can direct history, shape our environment and mold our lives, and not the other way around.

I believe that wherever and whenever this human spirit is in evidence—whether it is a prisoner striving to be heard, someone in a concentration camp determined to live, or a laborer executing tasks with hope and confidence in the future—it is cause for celebration of life. Whenever we are striving to remold a misshapen world to our higher visions, or simply living in dignity in spite of circumstances, we are at our very best. The human spirit, dedicated to life and beauty and good, is not dead, in spite of all that we hear to the contrary.

When I was first teaching, I was determined to promote in my students an active imagination. I remember in particular an activity that we all loved which we called

"Balloons to the Moon." This is what we did: Each child received a balloon which was filled with helium, then tied, and had attached to its end a postcard with a message on it. It read something like, "Whoever finds me, please put me into a mailbox. I'm part of a very exciting experiment and need your help to complete it. Thank you for your kindness."

The balloons were all released in the air and the children watched as each lifted and disappeared from sight. The postcards were stamped and had a return address so that any that were found could be returned. It was sort of a contest to see whose balloon would go the farthest, and while the children's imaginations were given flight, we talked of weather patterns, local geography, and faraway places. We talked of the kindness of strangers—how people completely unknown to us might help out just to be nice. Most of the children imagined fantastic possibilities.

"Mine will catch a wind and make it to China," said one.

"Mine's going to sail over the highest mountain," said another.

"My balloon is caught on a telephone wire." There was always one!

"Well, here's another one, Johnny. Set it off!"

Imagination is the place where we keep the things that cannot be and yet we know they *are*. We sometimes assume that only children are especially in touch with this magical place, that adults have shed their innocence for a more tangible world. There are the vague recollections of a time in our lives when all things were possible, when the real world, with all its logic and restraint, was not yet upon us. Still, there are those occasional flights of fantasy, the daydreams, the journeys to faraway places. I've often wondered about the mystery of so much of the brain that lies fallow. Perhaps it is through our imagination that we

awaken some of its unknown potential. It is the one quality
that is invariably attributed to our most inspired, creative
people. George Bernard Shaw once wrote that "Imagination is the beginning of creation. You imagine what you
desire; you will what you imagine; and at last you create
what you will."

With just a little imagination we can shake loose from
the commonplace and make memorable some of those moments that are habitually the same. More and more it seems
that life is a creative achievement, something more than
just security and comfort. Imagination is being able to envision limitless possibilities and alternatives. It is seeking
new solutions to old problems. Each day offers new opportunities, new experiences—no day has ever been like
any other, and neither should our approach to it.

Find as many exciting ways as you can of doing mun-
dane tasks. Make cleaning house a symphony of movement for keeping trim. It could be anything from Mahler
to Michael Jackson to Sinatra. A well-choreographed samba
might be just the trick to bring a little flair and excitement
to doing the laundry. Try creating a spectacular pasta of
your own, rather than playing it safe with the usual pack-
aged noodles. It takes the same amount of time and it's a
lot more fun. Tap your creative instincts as often as possible
lest you begin to believe you have none.

From the accounts of prisoners of war who suffered
years of deprivation inconceivable to most of us, stories
are told of individuals who imagined an outer world in
every detail that they could summon. Dreams were born,
art was created, poems were written—all under the stark
and barren circumstances of their confinement. What an
incredible example of the power and liberating force of
imagination.

We have to take responsibility for our own boredom
and delve into the limitless opportunities that our imagi-

nations afford us. Whether in fashioning a masterpiece of art, or seeing a problem from a new perspective, the creative instinct is uniquely human and waiting within you to be tapped. So when your life seems emptier than it should, when it needs a healthy transfusion of vitality, use your imagination and tap your dreams. And, by the way, if you discover a lovely, light balloon one day, with a card attached, please send it on. I still dream of the wonderful places mine might have gone. And if I find yours, I promise to send it back posthaste!

I know it is close to heresy these days to admit to this, but I don't think it's any fun getting old. Yes, it's true that age has its privileges, and so it should, but let's face it, it has its share of disadvantages too.

I, for example, can't kick up my heels as I used to without getting a swollen ankle. In past years I could move through my home and office in a matter of seconds. Now it takes at least a third more time, and when I've finally arrived where I am going, I sometimes forget what I've come there for. I'm more absent-minded and more frequently rely upon others to tell me "what's-his-name's" name, or the title of the book I read last week, or the telephone number of my sister whom I've been calling for years.

I can't eat as heartily as I used to. The three servings of pasta that were generally preceded by a giant antipasto and followed by a huge piece of rum cake are now distant memories. Even a single serving takes hours to make its uncomfortable and noisy way through my digestive tract.

I can't see or hear as I used to. Without glasses, reading material needs the full extension of my arm to be deciphered. I'm noticing too that when I am listening to music alone in a room, the person entering always lowers the sound slightly.

I get more tired than I used to. An eight-hour day cries out for periods of rest; and, when I don't get them, I pay the price. I nod off sometimes during very important moments.

Of course, getting older does have its advantages. I was having a prescription filled the other day and the pharmacist offered me a ten percent discount. Movie theaters cut their admissions in half and the local eatery has special meals at one-third off after five and before seven. These little niceties are most gratifying, but I'd easily forego them for a few less aches and pains, a faster, more steady gait, or 20/20 vision.

It's difficult for me to honestly celebrate getting older. I know there have been many examples of people who never seem to age. George Bernard Shaw broke a leg while still fully functioning in his nineties—he fell out of a tree while pruning it! Grandma Moses did her best painting after she was one hundred years old. Our President, who is well beyond retirement age, seems to revel in the pressing duties of his office. It annoys me when I watch a fantastic-looking woman on T.V. expounding the joy of Oil of Olay on her wrinkle-free face, or a sprightly-looking gentleman telling me that he owes his vitality to Ex-Lax and has lived by it for lo these many decades! I have nothing against these products, but the implication for me is that we shouldn't show any signs of aging. I've tried that. It doesn't work for me.

We are told to forget that the human body does not function in top form forever. As with anything which has lasted 60, 70, or 80 years, there will be gradual wear and tear. Things will function less efficiently, they'll get clogged or stiff in the joints, or simply atrophy. This is a normal process and there is nothing wrong with it. Problems arise when we deny the process and become trapped in wishing it otherwise.

We now have a "Senior Citizen Month." It is proper that the aged should be so recognized and celebrated, but it seems odd to me to celebrate age. Perhaps it would be more fitting to honor those individuals who are still growing, productive and glowing *in spite of* their age.

I, for one, am determined to live as fully and as long as possible, despite the creaks and limitations. I may move more slowly but I'm determined to move. I may not be able to eat as much, but I refuse to relinquish the joy of food. I may develop any number of limitations, but I'm determined to keep my eyes and ears wide open, making room for every new experience.

I have great admiration for all those who have made peace with aging, accepted it as inevitable and risen above it. It takes strength, stamina, determination, and a keen sense of humor. That's what deserves celebration and recognition, not a birth date!

It is said that Methuselah lived to be 969 years old. This may be, but historically the maximum known life span for a human being has remained pretty much the same. We know of no one who has lived to be 150 and statistically few make it to 100.

There's always someone seeking a fountain of youth or ways of extending the life span. People have made millions from gadgets, vitamins, creams and special surgery— all of which hint at having the eternal secret. It is a fact that the average life span continues to increase. Scientists are diligently at work discovering ways of engineering our genetic or hormonal clocks, regenerating tissue and transplanting vital organs.

We seem to be more health conscious than ever, with the bottom line being a longer life. We have learned that if we exercise, eat intelligently—and give up smoking, we can live beyond our former expectancies.

Many of us would question whether life extension is a good idea. We're aware of the risks of uncontrolled population growth, finite food resources, and prolonging life for people who are no longer able to live it actively.

Other questions come to mind. Will greater longevity really improve the quality of our lives? Will it relieve a growing sense of discontent, loneliness and frustration? Will it help quiet our basic fears? Does a longer life necessarily mean a happier one?

Life is a fantastic gift, but I find few among us who are truly living it with dignity. Too many people bemoan their mortality and so few fill the time they have in life with joy.

I had many students in my years of teaching—young, attractive, intelligent and often with considerable wealth—who, when I would extoll the wonder of being alive, would roll their eyes as if to say, "What's so great about life?" They saw it, even at their young age, full of boredom, predictability, frustration, and problems, problems, problems!

At a recent talk I gave, I was confronted by a very angry person who said he just couldn't believe that I was sincere in the enthusiasm for life which I reflected in my television shows, my books and my columns. He suggested that one would have to be mad or a simpleton not to see the pain, despair and general sickness of our society. "What's there to be happy about?" he asked. "The world is full of pain and disillusionment and you're deluding us all by suggesting that one can rise above it."

The inference was clear that there is something not

quite right about people who openly profess a love of life. We must be lacking either in intelligence or in sincerity.

Again and again we hear life being put down. Rodney Dangerfield suggested that "Life is just a bowl of pits." Edna St. Vincent Millay said, "It is not true that life is one damn thing after another . . . It's one thing over and over." Kathleen Norris said, "Life is easier to take than you think; all that is necessary is to accept the impossible, do without the indispensable and bear the intolerable." Often quoted are the words of Thoreau, who said, "The mass of men lead lives of quiet desperation."

I hear these sentiments repeated in countless situations, as if life were a test of endurance. My question then is, "If life is such a drag, why are we so determined to extend it?" Sometimes I feel like an endangered species— so unique that I seem to continue to find inspiration in words such as those of Anne Frank: "In spite of everything life is good," and naively maintain that waking up each morning is a miracle.

Lest anyone think me hopelessly lost in my own wonderland, I recognize also that there is a darker side to life. For those who choose to view it mainly from this perspective, life may well seem like one overlong ordeal. Why indeed would we work so hard to prolong an existence of pain and fear and disappointment?

Certainly no one lives free of these things, but they represent only one side. There is also another side, a lighter side, of joy, hope, trust, laughter, beauty, wonder and love. Perhaps the good life is in learning to balance the two, remembering to let go of the darkness as soon as we have learned from it, while we continue to welcome the light.

I'm all for extending life, but I wonder if it might not be more important to first find ways of living our lives with more quality and dignity before we become obsessed with extending them.

A
Passion
for
Learning

George Bernard Shaw said it best when he wrote, "Life is no brief candle for me. It is a sort of splendid torch which I have got hold of for a moment, and I want to make it burn as brightly as possible before handing it on to future generations." Each of us bears a torch. We must keep it lit. The hope for tomorrow is to pass on blazing torches now!

I can't tell you how many graduations I've sat through in the last three decades of being a teacher. I've seen thousands of students receive their diplomas. I've listened to hundreds of speakers encourage them to "sail off into the challenge of tomorrow." I've watched as celebrities were given honorary degrees and alumni enthusiastically extolled the virtues of the "good ol' Alma Mater." I've observed parents desperately trying to locate their children among the assembly of young people, and swelling with pride as their child's name was pronounced (or mispronounced) by the President.

I've listened attentively as the valedictorian has given the class commencement speech, assuring the audience with trembling but practiced tones that this class would "make the world safe for democracy and find solutions to the economic and social ills endangering this greatest of all countries."

After a few hours of such continuing excitement, the ceremony comes to an end. The professors turn in their borrowed robes and wish their students well for the last time. The graduates have their pictures taken and are whisked off to homes and restaurants for festivities, and the custodians are alone on an empty campus. Left to fold the chairs, disassemble the platform and clean up the dropped programs and confetti, they grumble that the next commencement is just a few months away.

Graduation ceremonies certainly fulfill a very important function. Aside from being a mark of achievement for the graduates, they are also an assurance to the society about to receive them that they have acquired certain basic skills.

What continues to disturb me over the years is that we are not in agreement about what constitutes an educated person. Should we assume that the curriculum we prescribe for our young people prepares them not only for a complex and changing world, but also how to relate to other human beings?

What about faith and inner calm? What about happiness and enjoyment of living? What about courage and the conquest of fear? What about peace of mind, the ability to give and receive love? What of confidence, self-respect and self-discipline? What about hope for the future and contentment in later years? Where does this learning fit into the definition of the intelligent human being? Perhaps we have for too long believed that such things are not in the domain of public education, that people come by them naturally and develop them on their own time in their own way.

Declining achievement in our nation's schools has pointed up the need to reinforce basic skills. It is an understandable reaction to a very real problem. The danger lies in our overreacting and promoting efficiency and competency as the only true objectives of our educational system.

Somewhere along the way we need to reinforce the idea that we make decisions based on feelings as well as facts. Education's ultimate objective—that we grow and become the best person we can be and help others do the same—is only partially served by teaching the three R's. This requires us to expand our definition of education, not constrict it.

Sometimes after a graduation I leave alone, after the custodians, a bit concerned for our young, *educated* graduates—those who, I am told, will become our leaders. Have we done them justice if we've prepared them only to be skilled scientists, doctors, lawyers, teachers, engineers, and computer experts? Will the education we've given them sustain them in an insecure economy, a world on the brink of annihilation, a society charged with intimidation, suspicion and uncertainty? If not, we may have presented them with a degree which will serve them for little.

I'm still not sure what the truly *educated* person is, but I'm certain he's not dependent upon years of formal schooling. We will have been only half educated unless we have acquired survival techniques, a sense of human dignity and worth, an appreciation of life, the ability to give and receive love, the knowledge of how to use our limited time wisely, and the determination to leave the world a better place for our having been in it.

In 1973 I wrote a book which has remained my favorite published work, *The Way of the Bull.* The title was taken from a Zen Koan which told of a young man who went in search of the bull of wisdom. When he found him, he tied the bull to a tree in the backyard, thinking that in this way it would be his forever. Of course, in the morning the bull was gone. Wisdom is not so easily obtained. The book deals with my search, the people I met, the philosophies I encountered and what I learned from it all.

To each of us, at certain points in our lives, there come opportunities to rearrange our formulas and assumptions—not necessarily to be rid of the old, but more to profit from adding something new. Anthropologists tell us that we are indelibly marked and easily identifiable by the culture in which we are raised. We carry this imprint in the way we talk and walk, even by our posture. But we are distinguished also in our human ability to adapt to new ways and learn new things—to synthesize the familiar with the unfamiliar.

Much of what I was taught in the Eastern world has stayed with me. Aside from what personal value it has for me, like all learning, its greatest value is in being shared.

For instance, happiness, in the Eastern world, has little to do with acquiring material things which we so often use as a measure of a person's worth in our culture. Asians find happiness in the recognition of what one already has, and the development and full appreciation of it.

They believe that each person is perfect as is, but must work to reflect that perfection. They believe that a life lived fully is one that is being lived in the present. Most of us live too far into the future, or weigh ourselves down with regrets about the past. The only true value is to be found in the here and now. Much of our unhappiness stems from our tendency to live in the past or future, both of which are illusions.

Living fully each moment, at the moment, means living with enthusiasm and spontaneity. It is not only learning the exciting possibilities available to us in each moment, it is learning to create them, as well.

To believe in oneself is also an essential aspect of Eastern philosophy. It's not an unfamiliar idea in our part of the world either, though my experience has been that many of us don't really value ourselves as much as we should. We think that life would be better if we were someone else. We undervalue our talents and question our worth. We are hesitant about accepting a new challenge because we convince ourselves that we haven't the resources to meet it.

We see time spent on self-understanding as useless, even selfish. We are more frightened than challenged by our potential. We understand that we are only able to share the resources we have, but continue to feel guilty about spending the time necessary to develop them.

Asian wisdom suggests that we live in attentiveness, always open and fully aware. This requires us to listen without preconceptions, watch through unprejudiced eyes, recognize, as the Buddhist says, that a frog lodged in a well cannot ever understand the limitless expanse of sky.

New learning and perceptions come from many surprising sources. Our personal world may seem vast, but within the perspective of a universe we are all like the frog in the well—so small, so limited, so unaware of the whole. Our challenge is to break out of our limitations, self-imposed or otherwise, and accept the fact of our limitless self, vitally interacting in a limitless universe. How sad is the story of the caterpillar who looks up at the butterfly and exclaims, "You'll never get me up there!"

There is so much of value that we as Westerners can learn from Eastern thought. We are seeking the same things—self-knowledge, personal growth, inner peace—things which are attainable in many ways.

Our attitudes and philosophies fan out in an unlimited number of directions and so affect many thousands during our lifetimes. We truly have an obligation to become the best possible human beings we can. Any new learning which will aid us to attain this goal is a benefit to everyone. It may be our only hope of rising out of the well and joining the butterflies.

One of my happiest childhood memories is going to the local library after school on Thursdays for story hour. Our library had a small garden patio. There we kids assembled in a semicircle on the grass. Promptly at 3:30 P.M., the children's librarian appeared with a handful of books under her arm. She would sit on a small chair, greet us happily and begin her readings. What a magical time we had. It was there that I first became acquainted with Hans Christian Anderson, the Brothers Grimm, Lamb's *Tales of*

Shakespeare, Swift's *Gulliver's Travels;* and of course, wonderful episodes of Lewis Carroll's *Alice in Wonderland.*

I would never have known these great works if it had not been for Miss L. She was a trained, professional librarian. She loved books. She shared them as treasures.

As I grew up, it was this same person who dissuaded me from attempting to read every book from A to Z in the library. She taught me the difference between poor and great literature. She convinced me that libraries housed trash along with masterpieces; and, if I tried to read all the books, there would be no time for the truly great volumes.

For a start she gave me Mark Twain, Charles Dickens, Pearl Buck, Agatha Christie and Edgar Allan Poe. I'll be eternally grateful for her guidance and concern. For me, she opened worlds of words in which I've remained forever mesmerized.

Her method was a perfect example of teaching through modeling. Her abundant love of books was contagious and passed on to hundreds of us.

Recently, I was shocked to read that library schools are fast disappearing. There seems to be no longer any need, or perhaps not enough money, for trained librarians—especially children's librarians. Replacing them are computer experts and information scientists. Many libraries are closing their doors or having to restrict their buying due to severe budget cuts.

School libraries often have resources so inadequate as to be almost useless. This is so even though there is proof that early and easy access to books turns children into avid readers. Having interesting books at hand and reading them aloud to children makes readers of nonreaders. It's that simple. The American Reading Council has demonstrated that they have had close to 100 percent success among low income children in getting them to read and love books if they are provided with daily access to enjoyable books and magazines.

Another depressing step toward the inevitable is that our libraries will soon be run by computers. Certainly we will then have easy access to the books and information we desire in just a few seconds. But I wonder what will happen to the magic of storytelling in the garden, the sense of criticism and taste which can only be encouraged and passed on by a discerning, sensitive, knowledgeable person.

Meanwhile, the fact remains that we are adding one million illiterate teenagers each year to our already shocking number of nonreaders. Julia Reed Palmer, the executive director of the American Reading Council, recently wrote in *Publishers Weekly*, "Lack of access is a fact today for millions of American children who live in communities with no bookstore and who go to schools with no libraries."

There are some traditions we cannot afford to see eroded or economized. We hear enough about a future which is more and more hopeless without contributing in yet another way. A society which minimizes the value of reading or limits the accessibility of good reading materials is doing just that.

My childhood library still stands in an East Los Angeles suburb. It's a bit worn with age. The number of volumes hasn't increased greatly over the years due to continued financial cutbacks. The garden where so many of us first learned about the wonder between book covers is now being left to weeds.

A few weeks ago I had dinner with a very dear friend who is a public school principal. On this particular Friday night she appeared to be without her usual glow and bounce. Her gaze was distant and the sparkle was gone. She fell into a chair and let her head fall back and her arms dangle. "I'm beat!" she moaned. "What happened to you?" I questioned. "The usual." Then it all came out.

"One of the children fell and broke his leg. His parents are threatening to sue. Another parent came in screaming that I was prejudiced against her child because we hadn't placed him in a gifted class. There was a rabid squirrel on the school ground, and the custodian has threatened to quit unless the children stop messing up the restrooms. He wants them policed. How can I ask teachers to do toilet duty?"

I thought to myself, "This is the usual!?"

We live in a time and place in the world where there is education for all, regardless of income, social status or ability. Schools are set up to educate—to transmit the accumulated knowledge of the past while encouraging independent thinking, creativity and joy. Somewhere along the line we have also entrusted our schools with the teaching of values, physical and mental health, and even sex education. This we insist must go on, year after year, in classrooms of 30 to 36 students.

The only way we can relate to that would be to imagine having 36 children in our home and be expected to keep order, maintain interest, motivate them to read, write, spell, do arithmetic in order to become computer experts, gain a knowledge and appreciation of history, literature, music, art, and social and moral values! How many of us would take on that task? And if we would, could we do it eight hours a day, five days a week, for ten months a year? I constantly hear parents sigh after only three months of summer vacation, "Thank heaven they're going back to school."

I can recall very vividly the frustration I felt for the many years I taught second graders in a public elementary school. I loved my work. My only real problem was a feeling of isolation. I felt a real lack of appreciation for my needs—almost abandoned. The school board had more problems than they could handle. The superintendent was constantly being attacked by one concerned group or another. My principal was over her head in Band-Aids for parents and children alike. I could hardly expect these individuals to have time for a simple second grade teacher. And there were the parents. I remember working for weeks preparing for parents' night. I put up their children's work. I created all sorts of audio-visual aids to illustrate what we were doing to create a learning environment. I decorated the classroom, even arranged for coffee and cookies at my expense. This, in addition to a twenty-minute presentation which I had worked on for weeks. On the evening of parents' night three mothers showed up. Always the same ones.

Educating everyone is a difficult task because *everyone* includes children with educational limitations, low motivation, and social and emotional problems. Still, the educator plows ahead with a confidence bordering on naiveté. Perhaps that's what is needed.

I remember teaching in Asia where there is a no more revered profession. My students even stood at attention when I entered the classroom. Of course, I neither wanted nor expected such a thing and most of our teachers would agree. Nevertheless, the necessity to recognize and appreciate the role of educators in our society remains a vital consideration.

My friend and I discussed these things, and I'm pleased to report that after a quiet dinner with wine and good conversation, she was ready to go again. Her enthusiasm was back. Her eyes were alive.

But just a few days ago I heard that one of her teachers slipped on a toy and broke a rib. A child ran away. Her already bare bones reading program budget was cut. The roof was leaking. I hope, at least, that her custodian didn't quit, that the parents didn't sue, and that it won't rain. Then perhaps she can get on with what she was hired for—the process of education! May God bless the Educator.

•

Mark Twain once wrote that, when he was a boy of 14, he thought his father was so ignorant that he could hardly stand to have him around. But, he added, "When I got to be 21, I was astonished at how much he had learned in seven years."

Happily, as we grow and change, some of our most basic perceptions change as well. So it is with our images of father that we refine and focus as we grow wiser.

Unlike Twain, many people see their fathers as images of perfection, and soon learn that even pillars of strength have their vulnerabilities—that along with all their right answers and assurances, dads also have doubts and uncertainties; they are only human. We discover that our fathers are no more capable of perfection than we are. This might be a disappointment initially, but seems to bring us closer together in the long run.

When I was growing up, most fathers were out of the home much of the time. Children caught only glimpses of them in the morning or evening as they came and went to work. Father's role was mostly that of the strong, responsible, even punitive force in the family. "Just wait until your father gets home," was heard often. When father came home, he would mete out the required punishment. Seldom were fathers seen as warm, caring, nurturing parents—that was mother's role. Many children grew up hardly knowing their father as an individual. "I never see him," I'd hear from friends. "He's always too busy."

When I was a child, my father didn't fit this mold. Though he worked hard and was a good provider, he was also a real presence in our lives. He had no macho image to maintain. He was tender, warm and affectionate. Of course, he could also be firm when he needed to be. In fact, there was a look that came over him when he was disappointed or angry with our behavior that was our most dreaded punishment. We learned from his example, and were encouraged by his concern and involvement with us. We felt his active caring and love in many ways. These were his gifts to us, made all the more precious because they have stayed with us through the years.

Today's roles and attitudes are changing, and so is the image of Dad. Having worked with children and young people for all of my professional career, I have noticed striking differences in attitudes regarding fathers. It has been interesting, and heartening, to observe that over the past few decades fathers' primary roles have changed from determined providers to loving nurturers. We've finally learned that fathers have intuition and instincts toward being parents just as strong as those of mothers.

Happily for fathers and their children, the notion that real men leave the raising of children to Mom—that too much involvement in the upbringing of one's children somehow compromises one's masculinity—is becoming less and less a reality. There is a growing emphasis these days on the vital bond that develops between fathers and children. Studies indicate that this bond begins to form far earlier than we once imagined—even before birth. It has been demonstrated that babies in the delivery room show a decided preference for their father's voice over the voices of strangers. This suggests that in the previous nine months Dad was already making his presence known to his child. In addition, the old image of expectant fathers pacing nervously in a waiting room is being replaced by an image of two proud parents working and sharing in the profound joy of childbirth.

Men are realizing that they have a responsibility to provide for their children not only in material ways, but in emotional ways as well. They are also more than willing to make this commitment. Even fathers who are unable to spend as much time as they would like with their children are finding that the amount of time is not nearly as important as the quality of time they share. Warm, unhurried, joy-filled time together stimulates the mutual bonding and love so important to any relationship.

My father was a part of my life for over fifty years. He's gone now and though life goes on, no one can ever fill the void his death created. There can never be another Papa. It wasn't easy to say goodbye, but in a very real sense he'll always continue to live, through the joy of life that he taught me—his generosity, sense of humor and the many ways he made us feel so important, unique and loved.

I'll never be able to pay him back for all his years of giving, but he'd never expect to be repaid. It's good that we have a special day to honor fathers, but I'm happy I didn't wait to thank him until it was too late.

A
Passion
for
A Better
World

Too often our sensibilities are assaulted and bludgeoned by all that seems bad in the world—the T.V. bulletins of the day's horrors, the full, graphic story we get by watching the eleven o'clock news.

Why do we allow ugliness to assume such an overriding importance in our lives? If we don't cast it out with determination, it will surely blind us to all the bright reality around us. If only we could step out of our perceptual traps and see that beauty and goodness comprise at least an equal part of what there is. What a miracle would unfold in this world of negativity if we all subscribed to this one simple idea!

The man called the public library. The librarian reported that he sounded hesitant and frightened. He didn't want to give his name. After an awkward pause, he told the librarian that he'd heard about a program for non-readers. He said that he was calling for a friend. The librarian gave him all the information regarding the National Program for Adult Literacy. She encouraged him to help his friend to enroll at once, but as they talked, he admitted that he, and not his friend, was illiterate. He told her that his father had deserted the family when he was a child. His mother was sick and on welfare. He hated school and dropped out when he was twelve. Since that time he had worked at odd jobs to help support himself and his family. He never learned to read. Each time he tried to improve himself he was faced with a job application or impossible reading material. He was too embarrassed to admit he couldn't read and was forever relegated to coming to the same dead end street. He's reading now.

R. was in the eighth grade when she dropped out of school. She couldn't read a word. To support herself, she started with baby-sitting, followed by work as a maid at a local hotel and finally was promoted to hotel supervisor. She was so efficient that she was soon offered a much better paying job at a local hospital, but was afraid to apply because of her embarrassment at not being able to read. That's when she decided to respond to a T.V. ad regarding the local reading program. She was highly motivated and learned quickly. Larry, her program coordinator, told me recently that she is doing astoundingly well and presently she has a special goal: to be able to read her family Bible.

These are true success stories. They are only two of the 23 million American adults who are classified as functionally illiterate. That means that they do not have sufficient reading and writing ability to complete a simple job application or pass a driver's test. This is a problem that is being seen more and more as a crisis. The fact that 2.3 million individuals are added to the ranks of the illiterate each year justifies a certain alarm.

Unknown to many, there are actively successful programs to help alleviate this serious problem. They are offered free of charge and made possible through the efforts of volunteers throughout the country. The responsibility to administer these programs is passed on to each State by the U.S. Office of Education through the Governor's offices. The program is labeled The Adult Literacy Initiative. It's designed to make each individual community responsible for its illiterate population. Generally, the program emanates from local libraries.

At a ceremony recognizing the program's inception in 1984, President Reagan said, "Let us today resolve to roll up our sleeves and get to work, because there's much to be done. Across this great land, let those of us who can read teach those who cannot. Let the light burn late in our classrooms, our church basements, our libraries, around kitchen tables, wherever we can gather to help others to help themselves to the American Dream."

Volunteers all over the country have responded to the call. Diagnostic programs supervised by professionals are matching the needs of the nonreader with willing volunteers. This program is functioning, even within the walls of local prisons. Anyone is eligible.

Reading is essential for growth. It gives a whole dimension to our lives. It has been so since the first reading material was made available to the masses. It helps us to know and understand each other and our world better, to see beneath exteriors, to wipe out boundaries and distances. Thankfully there are those among us who are determined to achieve literacy for all.

Overcoming illiteracy in our country is a crusade that concerns us all. It deserves our support. Ignorance, especially as it applies to this growing segment of our population, is only served by our complacency.

Like so many other statistics that frighten or appall us, the trend toward greater illiteracy is seen as one more sign of our decay and disintegration. But while the doomsayers are marking our time, there are those who are stepping forward to reverse the trend—because they care.

What would we do without our dreams? How would we get through even one day without them?

Of course, I'm told that healthy individuals face reality head on, that to live with illusions is a very dangerous thing, that the world is a serious business and doesn't have room for dreamers. Well, I don't believe it. It's not a problem as long as we know the difference between illusion and delusion.

For many of us, reality can frequently be a bit too real. In fact, we are often tossed about by the whims of an incomprehensible, often cruel reality. We may be forced to face poverty, danger, illness, impending death, lack of love, loneliness—the list seems endless. Illusions can be a great help in handling these situations.

All of us live with illusions. They abound in places like Atlantic City or Las Vegas. I'm not referring to professional or compulsive gamblers, just the thousands of individuals sitting hopefully, hour after hour, at the one-armed-bandits, dreaming of hitting the jackpot. We know full well that the odds are against us, but we're sure the prize is just one more nickel, dime, quarter or dollar away. When asked why we do it, we say that it's just a form of recreation, that gambling is fun. But in the back of our minds is the newspaper story about the person who last year hit the million dollar jackpot. So we stay in the noisy, smoky room and try to stick it out. No real harm done—in fact, we are quite ready to do the same on our next visit.

It is often the hope of finding that certain someone that keeps the single people going to special bars, church socials, community events. Without these activities, which suggest that someone may be waiting at the very next turn, they might never break free from their past. That kind of illusion can't be too wrong.

I have a good friend who has a terminal illness. Not long ago she was told that her condition would worsen progressively. She had a dream, not a delusion, that getting back to her friends, family, job and old lifestyle would give her the additional momentum she needed for life. So far she's been right, much to the amazement of her physicians.

As a poor kid growing up in a Los Angeles ghetto, I had dreams of going to college and becoming a teacher— a seemingly impossible desire considering our financial condition. Mama, who had her share of dreams, was always more of a realist when it came to the dreams of her children. She wanted me to become a barber. "People will always have hair," she'd argue logically. "It keeps growing. They'll always need a good barber. You can't fail."

I was a stubborn kid and refused to relinquish my dream. I found a way to realize it. After five years of higher education, I became a teacher with the monumental salary of six thousand dollars a year. Mama was quick to point out that, figuring the price of haircuts, I'd have made a lot more than that and after much less preparation. Are mamas ever wrong?

I can't even imagine a world without those dreamers who have the feeling that things will be better tomorrow. With that feeling comes a sort of self-fulfilling prophecy and causes us to work actively to make things better.

I'm not suggesting that we all start living an illusion, but it's an interesting psychological finding that one hundred percent realists are often among the most depressed persons in our society. I'll take healthy illusion any day. If our dreams cause us to become active seekers and partakers of life, setting up the necessary contingencies for making things happen, then they can be positive forces which are conducive to happiness and growth.

We might learn a lesson from Snow White. She dreamed that someday her Prince would come. But in the meantime, in place of moping around, she had a good life with the Seven Dwarfs!

I had a student who is severely physically handicapped. She was born with cerebral palsy, which has affected all four of her extremities. Her muscles are tense and require an inordinate amount of energy to control. She has a wheelchair over which she takes command and pushes around with determination as often as she sits in it. She's an attractive girl. She has a brilliant mind. Without asking for any special advantages she has managed to climb the educational ladder to a graduate program in special education with a top grade point average. She is determined to dedicate her professional life to making the world a better place for the many individuals like herself.

During the day she works full time as a high school teacher. At the end of the day she drives herself to the university in her specially equipped automobile and takes evening classes. She then goes home and prepares for her next day's classes as well as does her homework. Never have I heard her complain or ask for any special considerations.

She is only one of many such impaired individuals I have worked with during my thirty years of interacting with the disabled. It has always seemed to me that, benevolent as we claim to be in our society, we should want to make life as easy as possible for such individuals, recognizing the almost insurmountable physical and emotional problems they must deal with in their daily lives. But every time I speak with my student she relates another horror story which indicates that prejudice, ignorance and avoidance of the handicapped as a group are still rampant in our society.

For example, when she told a rehabilitation counselor that her professional goal was to earn a Doctorate in Education, he told her that for her to strive for such an exalted goal was unrealistic. "Why," he added, "even I don't have a Ph.D. . . . "! We have a long way to go.

Another time when she was being interviewed for a teaching position, even though she had scored in the top ten percent on the written examination, had completed all the requirements with honors, and had proven her ability in her practice teaching and field work assignments, one of the interviewers took her aside and asked, "Why are you so determined and stubborn about getting a job? With the seriousness of your handicap you could apply for total disability and never have to work a day in your life!"

Most recently she caused quite a stir when she entered a gourmet restaurant with some friends. Even though, with elbows planted firmly on the table, she can get food to her mouth without too much mishap, the maitre d' was totally taken aback. His attitude reflected his disapproval that such a person should consider defacing his elegant establishment. She had to patiently assure him that all he had to do was to bring food and drink—she would do the rest.

A day seldom passes when she is not submitted to such demeaning, condescending experiences. Often, it's true, people mean well. Still, it's amazing to me that she is able to survive these situations and still maintain a sense of human dignity as a woman, and an unyielding sense of determination.

She is only one of the many thousands of handicapped—some blind, some deaf, some paraplegic—who must deal with this attitude daily. We sometimes seem to forget that they are people too. They vary as much as the nonimpaired. Some are efficient, strong and self-reliant. Others are careless, frightened and dependent. It seems that we should at least be able to allow these individuals to make their own statements without having to deal with our preconceptions. Few of them ask for special considerations. They ask only for the same understanding, caring and compassion we would give to any human being.

Many of us still react negatively to differences, physical or otherwise. We avoid those individuals who do not meet *normal* standards, who move differently, who look different, speak differently, use canes, wheelchairs, or braces. We forget that these are only external things and are the least important facets of the individual. We fail to get beyond the cosmetic and directly into the heart. When we do allow ourselves to do this, we find a person there like ourselves—who loves, cries, laughs, knows frustration and loneliness and desperately wants to be appreciated for what he or she really is. It is at this point that the human connection, a connection which goes beyond the impairment, becomes possible.

Each year we read about or see television coverage of natural disasters: floods, tornadoes, hurricanes, earthquakes. We are appalled by the devastation they create and are amazed by the ability we human beings have to rise above them, to reenergize, to reassemble our resources and go on living.

For instance, each summer California dries up. Those of us who are natives prefer to call it California's "golden period," a time when the state's rolling hills become golden and beautiful because of the tall dried grasses. Of course, the slightest spark can bring on a roaring inferno of seven foot high flames which, when fanned by the summer winds, can devour anything in its path. Gallant fire fighters battle the flames for weeks on end, often successfully, but at times helplessly, while the fires explode trees and houses, kill animals and plant life—anything in the way.

Recently I spoke with some friends who live in one of these dry rural areas and were still shaken as they described "that night the fires came." They stood outside their home watching the flames surround them in the night sky, moving closer with each moment. They told of the intense heat and ashes, and of the oppressive winds taking their breath away. There was the dreaded sound of the police and fire vehicles sent to blare out the news of a necessary evacuation, and then the numbing · scene of friends and neighbors gathering up their families, pets and valuables, abandoning their homes to the approaching flames.

They described how in the midst of this tragedy and pain there was also a common concern and understanding among the neighbors. Volunteers came from everywhere to evacuate houses, search the neighborhood for each other's children and do what they could to save property.

Everyone and everything seemed to move silently and quickly through the darkness as the roads filled with vehicles heading for safe ground. The warnings continued through the night as the sky blazed a darker red.

Finally my friends followed their neighbors. They gathered their two dogs, two cats and two horses. They went into their home for what might be the last time, trying to decide what to take with them. They looked about them at the things they'd collected and loved and cared for all these years: works of art, furniture, mementos—no time to take any of them. A lifetime of accumulated memorabilia, and nothing to do but shut the door and leave it all to fate. There was only time to gather up some valuable papers, rush out the door and not look back.

It was interesting to hear what people took as they frantically escaped to safety. One woman took her grocery discount coupons. A man took a box of tools (he was determined to build again). Some took family albums, kitchen utensils, antique furniture, letters. One man even took his television set. Another took his daughter's favorite toys— the teddy bear she couldn't sleep without and her Cabbage Patch doll. This, he felt, would give her some continuity amidst all the uprooting.

It would be an interesting exercise for us all to ask ourselves what we would salvage if we had only a few moments to gather things. We would certainly learn a great deal about ourselves.

If such disasters have any value, it must be in causing us to look deeply into what is truly important in life. Too often our worth as individuals is determined by how many things we possess and what their monetary value is. We can become so attached to our things that we sometimes find ourselves controlled by them. We forget that things are usually replaceable.

I recall time after time, while on my world travels, visiting lands where natural catastrophes were a way of life and had taught the local people well. Why build big houses in places where monsoons would likely take them into the sea? Why accumulate things which will only have to be packed and moved? How much wiser to invest in more permanent and vital things such as family and friendships.

People in the aftermath of catastrophic events often

seem to have a strange sense of exhilaration. Perhaps it is because they find they can survive a threatening situation, or perhaps it is the realization that they are not alone— that there are those who would stand by them in time of need. Whatever the insight, it's a pity that we must sometimes suffer tragedy in order to learn the real values.

"Don't ever waste," Mama would say. "Think about all the starving people in the world." Was there ever a mother who didn't say that? I must admit that thinking of starving people in the world didn't help my appetite. In fact, with my dish full of food, I couldn't imagine what she was talking about. It was not until years later when I traveled the streets of the world that I began to understand a little about the effects of poverty and hunger.

We in America are among the best fed people in the world. We return mounds of uneaten food in restaurants, throw out great quantities in our garbage cans, and allow it to go to waste in our refrigerators. We seldom permit ourselves to feel hunger pangs. Why should we?

We have short-order food stands around every corner, well-stocked supermarkets everywhere, and restaurants of every degree of splendor specializing in varieties of cuisines. Most of us have some money in our pockets to purchase these things when we choose. Why should we concern ourselves with hunger?

The World Bank estimates that a quarter of the human race in the world today is chronically undernourished. One out of every four human beings will go to bed hungry tonight and more than half of these are children. We don't have to go out of our country to find hunger. All we need do is look in at any food kitchen from Los Angeles to New York, from Detroit to Dallas. If we study the greater picture, we find that half the population of all developing countries is hungry. One out of every two people in Benin, Cape Verde, Gambia, Mali, Somalia, Niger, and many other countries is starving. Remote places . . . almost unreal . . . not very pleasant . . . easy to forget.

There is no shortage of food in the world. There is sufficient food, I've read, to provide two pounds a day for every living person on earth—surely enough for the maintenance of life. But having food available is just not the whole problem. If it were, there wouldn't be any hungry people in the United States.

I recall my wisecrack answer as a child when I was told that I had to eat everything on my plate because of the starving children in Africa. I'd mumble over my plenty, "Well, why don't you wrap it up and send it to them." I can't tell you how brilliant I thought my solution to be. If it were only that easy.

World hunger is not like an immediate crisis to which we respond once and it disappears. It is an ongoing problem. Our role in attempting to alleviate it raises moral, political and practical questions— questions that governments, as well as individuals, are not always willing to face. Although it's not difficult to reach the conscience of anyone who has seen the anguished faces and the distended stomachs of starving children, it is sometimes too remote a problem for others to concern themselves about.

Few can question the humanitarian tradition in most of the world. An article or news broadcast about a family in need always produces immediate and positive responses. No one truly desires anyone to suffer or starve. After all, we are all members of the human family and we exist together on a very small planet. The pain, desperation and agony brought on by hunger cannot be ignored. Hunger continues to initiate the most violent wars. It has been known to topple the strongest governments.

Franklin Delano Roosevelt reminded us that, "True individual freedom cannot exist without economic security and independence. People who are hungry and out of a job are the stuff of which dictatorships are made."

There is no simple solution for ending poverty and hunger in the world. It seems shocking to me that it has been with us for so many centuries and still many of our our great educators, scientists, physicians and religious leaders do not accept this horror as a number one priority and humanity's most immediate challenge.

There is something that each of us can do if we are willing. Finding ways to become involved is a good beginning.

A few years ago I was invited to a local high school for a very special day that had been weeks in the planning. It was called International Day and everybody—students, teachers, administrators and parents—participated. It was a school which had a very diverse ethnic enrollment and this was to be a day to celebrate that diversity. In a central area of the campus, foods from around the world were prepared and proudly displayed. Many students wore clothing that was traditional for their native country. There was Latin music in one area, sitar music from India in another, rock in another, music from the Middle East in another, and taking their turn on a makeshift stage were four very elegantly dressed Korean girls doing a traditional dance. There was a special magic in the air that was beautifully reflected in the smiling and proud faces of all who participated.

The teachers and administrators were glowing as they observed their student body milling together, watching, learning, celebrating—such a contrast to the tight-knit ethnic groups that usually dominated the scene. The objectives of this event were clearly to increase the students' awareness and appreciation for other cultures, but as I observed and joined in the spirit of this day, I felt a far more important cause was being served. There was a sense of togetherness that was felt and spread by all. Prejudices and animosities were momentarily forgotten. Perhaps for the first time, some of these young people could emerge from their stereotypes and truly sense the pride that comes from varied heritages rich in tradition.

I'd like to believe this day was something more than just a diversion from the classroom. From the interaction I observed, I would judge it was a total triumph for human relations. I'm enough of a realist to know that ingrained habits and prejudices are not so easily changed. The distance between these groups could not be spanned in a single day. More days like it would certainly help, however. Many of the students no doubt reflected the concerns of their adult models. After all, the school was only a microcosm of the larger community, which had been, and still is, struggling to adjust to its growing ethnic diversity.

Enjoying friends and getting along with others is one of the most basic of human needs. I have never known a time when qualities such as friendship and consideration for others were not considered among the greatest of human virtues. H.A. Overstreet stresses this in his statement that, "A person is not mature until he has both the ability and the willingness to see himself among others and to do unto those others as he would have them do to him."

Yet, often when we are confronted with change or unfamiliar situations or people, our instinct is to withdraw, or even in extreme cases lash out against them. The constructive, dynamic potential that change can bring seldom occurs to us when we place such a premium of familiarity and conformity. The things which make us different should be cause for celebration. Think of it! Each of us is unique among all the varieties of life, and in so many vital ways.

When Robinson Crusoe discovered Friday, though they had vast and varied differences, the joy of their shared company removed any barriers that might have come between them. They became understanding friends. I believe that we sense the truth in their story. It is the same sense that tells us how beautiful it is to see young children who have not yet learned the *importance* of things like skin color, shape of eyes, or a different language.

A good friend recently told me of a case in point. Her daughter is presently attending a first grade class which is predominantly black. She loves her school and her friends. Recently she was sitting at the dinner table with her parents. Out of the blue she said, "Can I have a baby sister? And please, can she be black?"

Once we all were children. What happened?

A
Passion
for
Celebrations

Life is meant to be a celebration! It shouldn't be necessary to set aside special times to remind us of this fact. Wise is the person who finds a reason to make every day a special one.

Traditionally the start of every new year is a time for letting go of the past, wiping the slate clean and renewing our hope in a future, both immediate and distant. We are of course most receptive to anything that strengthens our faith in tomorrow. After all, that's where we will spend the remainder of our lives. Our tradition of forward thinking also includes a vision of a better life for generations yet to come.

So for the sake of continuity and posterity we invest the future with our best intentions. We try to remain hopeful for tomorrow's children and their children. But we are continually reminded from many sides of dark clouds on the horizon. Hope and apprehension for the future are forever in a running battle. We are told that the future will not be a very nice place in which to live; but a different impulse tells us that where there is life there is still hope.

I've often thought that we allow our past to speak too loudly in its implications for our future. Though very often accused of being too optimistic and even Pollyannaish, I am always more willing to look for positive signs than for inexorable doom.

There's a lot of pessimism out there and I'm not buying it. In fact, I'm sick of it. It's hard for me to understand people who say things like, "I'm not bringing a child into this troubled world"; or, "Better we should end it and start over again."

From my vantage point, the world still has just as much chance at Utopia as it does at Armageddon. Besides, like William Faulkner, if I must choose between a life of pain and suffering and no life at all, I'll take the pain and suffering anytime. No matter how miserable people tell me that existence is for us, I'll never be without hope. I haven't learned how to lose it yet.

When I so often say that we all have unlimited potential, I mean exactly that. I feel certain that the most stunning novel is yet to be written, the most awesome building has yet to be built, the greatest symphony is yet to be composed, the tastiest dessert is yet to be dreamed of. There are planets and stars to be investigated and visited—a whole, as yet undiscovered, universe will continue to stagger the imaginations of a thousand more generations. There are breakthroughs still to be accomplished in virtually every field of human endeavor.

From my perspective, I plan to learn from the past and not suffer because of it. Like many before me, I see a renaissance just ahead and I want to be part of it. It's only natural that I wish to join those whose main purpose is to pass along to another generation the accumulated knowledge and inspiration of the past.

It's really not a lot to ask. We have witnessed so many fantastic things and we know with our hearts and our minds that miracles do happen. I ask only that we believe in the simple proposition that it is continued hope which sustains life. And hope arises from the knowledge that we are living in a time of abundant new beginnings. That's cause enough for celebration.

All of our holidays have one thing in common: a sense of gratitude we share for something or someone. We are thankful to God, to Mom or Dad, or to those who were dedicated to a principle or a cause greater than themselves. The celebration of national holidays was impressed upon me early in life. I especially loved the ones that earned me time off from school. I had a guilty feeling, however, that I should observe these special days by celebrating and by commemorating what they stood for. Too often they became a cause for a vacation instead.

The Fourth of July was always given special significance in my home because my parents were immigrants. To them, all the clichés about coming to the land of opportunity and freedom were true. Mama and Papa often told us of the long ocean voyage that brought them to a new life; of the Poles, Russians and Greeks who were crowded together with them; of the mixture of hope and fear written on all their faces; and of the joy of first viewing the Statue of Liberty. They clearly remembered spending anxious hours at Ellis Island, then being ushered into a rush of human activity, which, to their amazement, was a typical day on the streets of New York. From there it was many days on a train through the heart of the country to the West Coast—a place that only a year earlier was as distant and unreachable as any spot on earth could be.

Reliving those days were Mama and Papa's way of celebrating a dream of a better life come true. The Fourth of July always seemed a fitting occasion to recall their great adventure—there were enough twists and turns and interesting people to make it a grand story every time we heard it. Mama and Papa insisted that their children give thanks for being able to live in a land of such freedom and abundance. They seemed more patriotic than the parents of my friends who were born in America and often took their freedom for granted. My parents' gratitude was deeply felt, and they wanted their children to feel the same.

Today patriotism has become something to snicker at. But I continue to remember the human values and principles that are very much a part of our daily lives, even though they are often taken for granted.

We live in a country, for example, that has a tradition of welcoming newcomers to its shores. We regularly attribute America's greatness to the diversity of its people and to the piece of the world they brought with them.

We've also managed to maintain a sense of humor in our country. It's wonderful to be able to take time off from the serious business of living in the real world to find so many things to laugh at. We hold an undying affection for the people who make us laugh, especially in our darkest hours when laughter is most needed.

On one hand, we celebrate the world's oldest living Constitution and, on the other hand, we are ever restless for change and for finding a better way. We continue to honor the wisdom and foresight of those before us, but we also never forget that we are no less responsible for maintaining the principles of the Constitution. We are far closer now, for instance, to "All men are created equal," than when the Declaration of Independence was written. And we have every reason to believe that future generations will perfect the idea further.

I love the fact that Americans aren't afraid of criticism. We make no effort to hide our shortcomings. Neither do we try to close the book on our past so that we may forget a few of its sorry chapters. We always seem ready to challenge and reexamine the values that we hold out to ourselves and others. We do this as individuals and, no less, as a nation. In taking stock in ourselves, it's fitting that we celebrate our Fourth of July with the cheers, accolades and superlatives that we deserve. We have much to be grateful for.

I love the Fall. I think it's my favorite time of the year. There is a wonderful nip in the air. The trees become rainbows and the feel of soft wool sweaters is reassuring against the cold winds. It's a dormant time, a time for all things to rest for a while—except for humans. We go on and on. But even *we* are asked to sit back and take a moment to reflect, to review our labors and celebrate what is completed before Spring starts the process all over again. It's that time again for expressions of thanksgiving.

There's something wonderful about the celebration of Thanksgiving. It's such a uniquely American holiday. We hear repeated the stories of Plymouth Rock, Pilgrims and friendly native Americans. We talk about counting our blessings and make lists of those things for which we are thankful. We stop lamenting for a moment things we don't have and celebrate the things we do have.

I can still remember vividly, as many of us can, being in elementary school and preparing for Thanksgiving. We cut out turkeys and colored pictures of the first Thanksgiving feast. Then, happily, with feathered headdresses firmly set on our heads and our turkey cutouts in hand, we were released from school for a four-day holiday. For that, we were truly thankful.

I am amazed how well I remember our Thanksgiving preparations in Miss V.'s third grade class. Miss V. was a very special teacher—one of those you appreciate more in retrospect than at the time. The students thought her an oddball, but no one objected to being in her class. Not only did we do all the usual things for Thanksgiving, but Miss V. had some very special ideas of her own. She requested that we all make a list of the things we were personally thankful for. She told us that we'd be sharing these things with the class just before the holiday.

Though none of us expected much from this assignment, we all did as requested. When the day came we all sat down in a semicircle with Miss V. at the center. She asked for volunteers. Silence. Even in the third grade we had already learned that only fools volunteer. Finally, after an anxious silence, F., the class star, offered to share her list. She was grateful for her doll, her bicycle, her stuffed bear, etc.

Miss V. was furious. "Trivia!" she shouted. "Those

are all unimportant things. It's nice that you have them and you should be grateful that you do. But think of the important things we have to be grateful for!" We were all confused. What more important things could there be than our dolls, bicycles, and stuffed bears? Silence. One of our less brilliant classmates ventured a guess. "Turkey?" he asked. Miss V., not renowned for her patience, turned bright red and went into a tirade. "That's just another unimportant thing," she said shaking her head. "Now think!" Silence.

"Why do we really celebrate the day called Thanksgiving?" We all sat quietly, afraid to speak. "Because the Pilgrims landed on Plymouth Rock," the class genius volunteered again. "That's part of the reason but that's the historic reason. What should we be thankful for now?" she sighed deeply. Another silence.

"Well, I guess I'll have to help you. I'll start." We were in rapt attention. She started: "I'm thankful for my eyes that see, my ears that hear, my legs that let me walk, my arms that hold, my mouth that speaks, my mind that thinks. I'm thankful for all the beautiful things in the world and my ability to enjoy them. I'm thankful for hope and dreams and love." This was all too much for the class. We thought it was hilarious. Of course, no one dared look at anyone else for fear that we'd break up, but we heard a snicker here and there. Our fun was not long lasting, for it was now our turn to complete the assignment.

It was natural that most of us echoed Miss V.'s list. With serious faces, stifling laughter, we told each other that we were grateful for our eyes, nose, ears and so on. Some of the more daring class members even began to add things like pets, mothers and fathers, brothers and sisters, and God. But it was J. who changed the day. He was a very small, rather undernourished, shy, and quiet Latin boy. He had hardly been heard from during the year. In a rather quavering voice he said, "I'm thankful I can go to school and learn. Then, when I grow up I can get a good job and help my mother and father and sisters. Maybe then we can have a nice house and my mother won't be sad all the time and won't fight with my father." I remember that he stopped and looked at Miss V. for approval and added, "And I'm thankful for my ears and my eyes, too."

In a moment, Miss V. had him in her arms. She gave him the longest loving hug I had ever seen her give—she wasn't usually much of a hugger.

I can't speak for the other class members, but that scene stays vividly in my memory. I learned a little more in those few seconds about the real significance of Thanksgiving. It had a little to do with history but it was mostly about now.

Even today I know that my friends and family think I'm crazy, but like Miss V., I use the Thanksgiving meal as a special expression of thankfulness and encourage everyone else at the table to do the same. There are so many things we take for granted in our daily lives. Why must we wait until losing them to realize how thankful we should have been for them? I'd like to present a partial list of what I'm thankful for.

The miracle of life. The privilege of being alive, of waking up in the morning ready for a new day to be experienced with enthusiasm and vitality, the challenge that is mine to make the world a better place, both for me and for everyone else.

For people—each one unique, no two alike. Each with something special to contribute—those who agree with us and help us to grow, as well as those who disagree

with us, challenge us and help us to see
new possibilities.

For food—wonderful food, each morsel differing from any other. The odors of
chicken soup simmering on the stove, or a
roast cooking in the oven. The taste and
smell of basil, rosemary, crisp apples, ripe
peaches, freshly gathered tomatoes and
green peppers, onions and garlic.

For gardens—grass, vegetables or
flowers. Roses, orchids, daisies and forget-
me-nots. Carrots, potatoes, radishes and
corn.

For optimists, for they make all things
a possibility.

For pragmatists, for they keep us in
balance.

For romanticists, for they keep our
dreams alive.

For a future, and what is called
progress, in the hope that it might lead us
to solving the world's problems: hunger,
war, fear, suspicion, loneliness.

For the past—the fond memories of
how things were. Pre-television days
when we took time to talk to each other.
When things were made to last. When
there were real butchers, bakers and can-

dlestick makers in place of people who appear only when we "ring the bell for service."

For our country, for the United States of America, imperfections and all, which is still the freest land in the world. Where we can worship freely, choose our own leaders and live an existence mainly of our own choice.

For good health: the superb feeling of having full power to use our mental and physical resources to the maximum. And if we aren't as well as we might be, to use what we have and make it do.

For family and friends, for they offer us the needed consistency and loving support that make it possible for us to continue to risk, and fail, and keep trying. It's good to know that there is someone close by who cares, forgives and accepts.

Our society has provided us with a multitude of things to be thankful for. At the same time it has made some of us too sophisticated for a simple, heartfelt expression of gratitude. A strange paradox.

The original Thanksgiving was a celebration of abundance made more meaningful by memories of scarcity and hardship only a short time before. We tell and retell the Pilgrims' story to carry forward the spirit of that celebration. We do this in the hope that each Thanksgiving we will open our hearts and our minds, even if only for the day, and appreciate the miracle of our existence—and appreciate especially having each other to share it with.

Each year we set aside one day for the celebration of love. We send cards and make phone calls. We buy candy and flowers as offerings for those we love. Even these token gifts we sometimes choose grudgingly. I'll never forget an experience I had in a stationery store once just prior to Valentine's Day. I was among many people looking through cards covered with hearts and cherubs and red bows.

A woman squeezed herself among us and started groaning about what a nuisance Valentine's Day is. The whole thing was just another commercial exploitation to her, yet she felt compelled to get a card for her lover. Then the cards were either too sentimental or too stupid. When I suggested she might write her own she replied, "Are you kidding? Who has the time for such . . . . . .?"

This heartwarming experience was almost immediately followed by another. A young woman was complaining that she had been sent by her boss to buy a card for his wife. "If my husband couldn't take the time to personally buy me a card I'd kill him!" she said angrily. There I was, surrounded by hearts, cupids, and loving sentiments, and suddenly the place was a war zone.

We seldom give any serious thought to human love on this special day. I've often thought that we should spend at least as much time studying the dynamics of loving each other as we do in acquiring any other skill. For various reasons, though, we don't do this. We say that love is indescribable. We say that it's unattainable; or, as with so many other things, we take it for granted. Some of the following might be considered, not in any definitive sense, but as simple expressions of a very complex subject.

The next time I have the urge to speak negatively or rudely to you, I'll swallow and be silent. Loving you doesn't give me license for rudeness.

If I can't be generous and supportive, I'll at least try not to stand in your way. Loving you means wanting you to grow.

I won't put my problems onto you. You have enough problems, I'm certain, and you don't need mine. My love should simplify your life, not complicate it.

I don't always have to be right. I can accept the fact that you are right as often as I am. Loving is sharing with each other. If I already know I'm right, I'll never profit from your insight.

I don't always have to be running the show. Loving is an ebb and flow. Sometimes I'll need to give in. At other times I'll need to take control.

I don't have to be perfect, nor do you. Love is a celebration for our humanness, not our perfection.

I can give up wanting to change you. If I want you in my life, the best thing for both of us is for me to accept you as you

are. After all, love is moving forward together in mutual growth.

I don't need to place blame. Since I'm
an adult who makes decisions based upon
personal experience, there is no one to
blame for a poor decision except myself.
Love puts the responsibility where it
belongs.

I can give up expectations. To wish is
one thing, to expect is another. One brings
hope, the other can bring pain. Love is free
of expectations.

To love is the greatest of human experiences and
sooner or later we all realize that without it life is empty
and meaningless. Love is always worth the effort, even if
it brings confusion, uncertainty and pain in the process.
A loving relationship should be a celebration all its own.
Let's use this special day as a reminder of that, and then
continue celebrating throughout the year.

A
Passion
for
Communication

One of the surest expressions of love is the sharing of thoughts and feelings. Loving others is to want to understand how they think and how they feel about themselves and the world they live in. Where words fail, it's comforting to realize how many other vital and eloquent ways we have of communicating with each other.

One of our mightiest human possessions is the word. Words have the power to build, to store and create, as well as tear down and destroy. We think with words, we organize our world with words, we communicate with words, we inform with words, we build relationships with words. Our worlds are very much limited by the words we use. Sometimes we become so caught up with words that we forget that they are just symbols for things, and we begin to see them as a substitute for the things they are meant to represent.

It's important to remind ourselves that words are just phonetic symbols put side by side. By themselves they're nothing. Most of the words we know were learned before we were six or seven years old, too early to fully analyze or understand them. These words were defined for us and we accepted them as presented. For example, if the significant people in our lives felt strong hate toward a particular person or thing, the words they taught us concerning these things became a part of our attitude as well. The words soon represented a constellation of thoughts and feelings surrounding those things. Soon we found that we were thinking and responding negatively to them. Of course, this couldn't be helped. Nevertheless, it was in this way that we learned what to hate or fear or avoid.

Just as we acquired the words for goodness, hope, optimism, joy and love, we learned also to attach negative symbols and discovered early the power of directing them where we pleased. We found that words could hurt. As a child, I can remember the standard retort for word bullies: Sticks and stones may break my bones but names can never hurt me! Occasionally this brought a rock or a stick my way, but it was more difficult not to feel the sting of such words as *dirty wop, skinny freak, dumb retard*. I wonder how many of us still feel the pain of labels that devastated us long ago.

Perhaps one of the great human tragedies is that few of us even stop to ask whether the words we think with and which cause us to feel so strongly are ours or simply echoes which continue to reverberate in our minds. If we stopped to redefine these words, we might discover that many of them are no longer relevant to the present. Words we learned as children may have prevented us from truly experiencing and understanding other persons or things as they really are. For many of us these words continue to serve in their capacity to reject, exclude and judge.

The great humanitarian-scientist, Buckminster Fuller, said that one of the most significant events of his life was when he stopped everything and wrote his own dictionary. He redefined words according to his experience, as what they represented in *his* reality, not that of others. This effect forced him to re-examine his values and reassess his attitudes. It gave him a far deeper appreciation of the power of words for the remainder of his life.

As adults we know that certain behavior is discarded early in life because it is childish and inappropriate. As wise adults we learn that certain words and labels should be discarded as well because they are hurtful or destructive, and if that means passing up the opportunity to tell the latest ethnic joke, then we are all the more fortunate for that insight.

There can be no word large enough to encompass the wonder of a human being. To judge others by a single label is to miss them entirely. As a child I may have been poor, or skinny, or Italian, or a number of things, but I was much more than each one of them. Thank goodness for those special individuals who learned to look beyond the labels and to know me as a whole person. It's not surprising that they turned out to be the people most worth knowing.

Words so often desensitize us. They can paralyze our senses as well as our better instincts. Words are powerful things which we too often take casually. They were created to help us give organization to chaos. But, unless we are careful, they become traps which lead us to apathy, hate and loneliness. We mustn't allow words to control us. They are our tools to enlarge, not narrow, our lives.

We all need to touch and to be touched. In his book, *Touching*, Ashley Montagu warns us that we cannot fully function and grow without being touched. Volumes of literature attest to the crucial importance of tactile stimulation to a newborn baby; in fact, studies indicate that brain damage, even death, may result from a lack of it. Dr. Montagu writes that this need for being stroked and fondled does not diminish with age. If anything, it increases.

This brings to mind a friend whom I shall call Cliff. He is a wonderful man, a devoted and loving father, and in the usual tradition of the American male, very restrained in any open display of affection. Though no one can question the love he feels for his five sons and they for him, it has not been their custom to be overtly expressive of their feelings for each other. When they greet each other they do so with a "Hi" and a handshake.

About a year ago Cliff suffered a severe stroke. The damage was extensive and irreparable. In addition to physical and mental impairment, there was an amazing change in his emotional makeup. A lifetime of developing a tough exterior was stripped away in the moment of extremity. In fact, the first time I visited him after the stroke, he gave me a tremendous hug. His eyes filled with tears. He no longer seemed to care about convention or what others might think of a man who would openly embrace another man. Even though he was left without speech, that one tender moment spoke volumes.

For the sons, much of what they cherished in their father was lost. But what they now discovered was a new, more gentle, loving person, one that had been hidden from them for all their years. Those who knew Cliff were saddened to see him incapacitated but touched also by this change that had come over him. From the oldest son who is forty-five to the youngest who is thirty-four, their father was still an important role model, but now teaching them that showing affection is a sign of strength rather than of weakness.

So many of us hesitate to touch and be touched. We have learned to substitute a peck on the cheek or an impersonal handshake for a warm embrace, a caressing hand. I taught a class entitled Love 1A, in which I freely advocated that my students be more physically expressive with their families and friends. Some of them felt this was a slightly unorthodox activity and were noticeably uncomfortable with the idea. They couldn't even hug their parents!

We found that many of us really needed to develop a more demonstrative way of expressing our affection, and that, for whatever reasons, people do find the prospect of physically reaching out to others to be difficult. Yet we learned that for those who are reticent, there is always the joyful discovery that their reticence can be easily overcome. There are so many willing individuals who would gladly be recipients.

Most of all we came to the conclusion that where words fail us in our efforts to understand and be understood, reaching out with a hug or gentle touch is often the most direct and eloquent form of communication we have. There is something very unambiguous about one person surrounding another in a warm embrace. It's difficult to misinterpret a loving touch.

I received a letter once from a husband who learned

the value of this kind of communication from the recurring arguments he had with his wife. "Our arguments tend to follow a similar pattern," he wrote. "It's always logic versus emotion. I try always to be perfectly rational while she tries to communicate her feelings. We get nowhere. I know deep inside that sometimes all I have to do is take her into my arms and if it doesn't end the argument, it at least helps us to talk *to* each other instead of *at* each other."

One of our most basic goals in life should be to become better friends and lovers, to draw ever closer to each other in all ways. Touch is the most intimate of our senses and in reaching out to others, the message is clear: I'm here, I'm close, and I care. What a pity that many of us wait a lifetime to discover this miraculous power.

The other day I received a very kind invitation to a dinner party. It came during a period when my life seemed particularly frantic. I attempted to explain this to the caller, but she was unable to understand. She insisted. She assured me that the evening wouldn't be strenuous and would include only a few other guests. I suggested that because of the pressures I was dealing with, I'd probably be very poor company, but she was determined not to take "no" for an answer.

To say no is difficult. But so is accepting no for an answer. Why is it that "no" always seems to infer a rejection or imply rudeness? We seem obliged all too often to say "yes" when we should be saying "no." But how to say it gracefully? More often than not our attempts are inadequate, so we participate in activities from which we receive little pleasure, spending hours at receptions we detest, with individuals who exhaust us. We do this to avoid seeming impolite, ungrateful or exclusive. We forget that we have the right to say no to anything that concerns our own person or time.

It seldom occurs to us that a no answer can be the most considerate and positive one we can give. Saying yes from a sense of obligation, fear of rejection or guilt makes no sense. It's degrading to us and unfair to others. To be present anywhere in body only, without will or spirit, wishing to be elsewhere, is an insult to all concerned. A "no" in such a situation is certainly a blessing to everyone.

I recently talked to a friend who told me that she has come to dread her daughter's invitations to dinner. She senses that her daughter sees these evenings as unpleasant chores. Rather than confront her with it, she pretends to be more gracious and enthusiastic than she usually feels. She says she does this to keep peace in the family even if it means continuing to play out this little charade. Though there are times when a no answer seems out of the question, it is also possible that the alternatives are worse.

For example, it seems wiser to risk a possible misunderstanding than to spend useless hours in boredom or resentment. If there is one thing we don't owe to anyone, it is our reluctant presence. If we are only saying yes from a sense of duty, the other person is always better off without us. It's certain that others can and will survive without us if we're not available. We're more replaceable than we think.

Children illustrate this daily in their play and it would be well for us to learn from them. Mary runs to Pete with great joy and enthusiasm and asks him to play. Pete doesn't share her joy and tells her so. Mary doesn't become despondent or fall into a deep state of gloom. She asks Joe. Instinctively she knows that there are others available somewhere who will meet her needs. Her life doesn't revolve around Pete. She seeks out other friends who would love to play with her. They think she's great.

When others produce feelings of guilt in us when we say no it might be well to let them know at once what we are feeling. Generally, pointing it out in a kind manner that we are feeling manipulated or hemmed in will usually be enough to get them to reconsider their behavior if they truly care about us.

It's apparent then that saying no can, in many cases, become an act of loving. In fact, relationships grow best within certain limits and structures, and a "no" now and then helps to clarify what these limits are. "No" at the right time can help others to better understand us and our special needs. It's something we have a right to expect from one another.

Life is too short for us to spend great chunks of our time doing things we'd rather not be doing. We should be less fearful of saying no. In the end, it may be the most loving thing we can say.

It seems to me that if there is ever going to be peace among humans, we can't wait for total agreement—we're going to have to settle for coexistence. Since truth is so often perceived differently by each of us, it can be no other way. For all those who have good reasons for a nuclear freeze, there are as many who feel it would be political suicide. Thousands feel that one candidate for public office is a savior, and as many are certain that he or she will lead us to ruin. I am certain that if someone were to ask us the color of a red rose at which we were all looking, there would be some who would see it not as red, but wine or purple or magenta, and be willing to argue the point to the bitter end.

Such minor disagreements can be responsible for losing friends, breaking up marriages, and on a more frightening scale, bringing on world conflicts. Why do we have to fully agree with people in order to continue to love and respect them? After all, an opinion about something or someone is simply an opinion, a unique way of viewing the world. Each of us has a very personal world view; but no matter how we see something, we as people have more intrinsic value than any single opinion. In fact, I make a point of seeking friends who have diverse opinions. They are the ones who are most often responsible for my changing attitudes. They keep me continually evaluating my beliefs. They are the ones who most challenge my mind and encourage my growth.

It is well to remember that a loving relationship need not be an agreeing one. We can continue to coexist in love as long as we keep dialogue going. Perhaps if you see something as white and I see it as black, there is a meeting point, a gray area, upon which we might begin to agree. From this point we can extend the parameters of agreement. In the end we might never fully agree but we can come to understand that there are many ways of seeing things.

One of the traps we frequently fall into is the idea that arguments are either won or lost, that right and wrong can always be clearly defined by force of argument. When we dig in and argue *the* truth, we are mostly looking only for confirmation of *our* truth. Uncertainty becomes weakness and saying that the other guy might be right becomes unthinkable when we are convinced of our own rightness.

We tend to adopt fixed attitudes in certain areas. We cling to the rightness of our views as if they were inscribed on tablets; and in the process, confine ourselves to the limits of our own experience. I've heard arguments between people escalate to ridiculous proportions simply because they refused to acknowledge the possibility of being wrong—as if such an admission would compromise their worth as human beings—as if the maintenance of a healthy ego required constant vindication of their views. Ironically, the opposite is true. People who work hard at being infallible will inevitably learn the price of their insistence.

When we unburden ourselves of the responsibility of being right all the time, we are free to learn from others. Just the simple admission that "I might be wrong," or, "You might be right," can work wonders in communication. Instead of standing alone in our rightness, we can draw closer to each other by discovering common beliefs and looking for a basis for agreement. Having the strength of conviction ceases to be a positive attribute when it interferes with people trying to find truth in their common experience. Besides, what does it profit you if you are right and you have won, but have lost a friend?

Complex disagreements may not be easily settled, but it is well to start negotiations free of assumptions of right and wrong. Better to start with the possibility that there is a little wrong in the most right of us and a little right in the most wrong of us.

There are some important words and phrases we seem to have great difficulty with. They're everyday words that get caught between our good intentions on one hand and our inhibitions or fear of rejection on the other. Take for example those two seldom heard but highly effective words, "I'm sorry." For many of us "I'm sorry," is a painful admission of a fault or imperfection. They imply, "I was wrong," and that's the part that seems to activate our defenses and keep us from speaking.

But "I'm sorry," doesn't need to be a vindication for one side or another. It's far more effective in making things right again than in showing who was wrong. Still, the words come hard, as if saying them reveals some weakness, some vulnerability.

Just a little thought on the matter tells us the opposite is true. Being vulnerable and able to say, "I was wrong," is one of the surest signs of strength. It informs others that we are sensitive to their pain or to their mood. It's far better than putting up walls and trying to maintain the myth of being perfect. The magic words, "I'm sorry," have unlimited power to heal and restore.

There are other phrases with which we struggle now and then such as, "Help me." This implies a need for someone else's strength right now. A need to be together right now. No matter how independent and self-reliant we become, we will always need others. They are a source of confidence when ours is faltering. By offering us another perspective, they can help us to see more clearly. But these things are not always freely given and must often be asked for.

We learned early in life that, "I can do it myself," was very rewarding. We were encouraged to be self-reliant and told that asking for help was a sign of weakness. We therefore find it difficult to say, "I need you." We still like to feel that we are in total control and hesitate to reach out for help.

"I don't know," is another little phrase that comes hard to some of us. It's a curious thing the way we often need to project an image of infallibility, of always having an answer for everything. We've all encountered people like that. For whatever reason they regard "I don't know" as a personal defect, as if each question or problem in life represented a challenge to their reputations.

In a poem entitled *The Rock*, T.S. Eliot tell us that, "All our knowledge brings us nearer to our ignorance. Where is the wisdom we have lost in knowledge?" Some of the wisest people I know have the fewest answers and the least amount of certainty. Perhaps they have found that true knowledge is not in the knowing but in the seeking. I'm always a little suspicious of any organization or philosophy or creed that has *the* answer for every question. I think it is more likely that others are struggling with the same problems and asking the same questions, and some questions may have no answers. As each of us seeks to find our own answers in life, "I don't know," might be the best place to begin.

The last of our underused phrases is really contained in part within the other three. It says what the others can only imply. The words are, "I love you." Why is it so difficult for some of us to say these three simple words? Why do we leave this phrase behind and regard it as a vestige of our earlier, more romantic selves? We come to believe that after a time love speaks for itself, that it is something implied by a relationship. "We've been together for twenty years. If that's not love, I don't know what is." And so, sadly, the words go the way of flowers and moonlight drives and holding hands at the movies.

We forget that even the most secure among us needs reassurance from time to time. We don't realize that sometimes the other person may be feeling more remote or disconnected, or that we ourselves are becoming more complacent in our relationship. Saying, "I love you," implies that "I don't take you for granted," that the force which brought you together still keeps you together.

The space that so often expands between people is so easily bridged with the right words at the right time. As relationships and the people in them inevitably change, it's important that we reaffirm that some things are constant. "I'm sorry," "I need you," "I love you," are powerful ways of reinforcing this affirmation.

• • •

Every culture shares a common repertoire of visual signals. Each time we make contact with others, whether for the first time or in a daily setting, body language can establish instant rapport. A whole array of clues and cues are on display.

Take smiles, for example. Such a simple yet telling act. There are some people who seem to think a smile is a major investment in human relations. They seem to be saying that a smile is risky business indeed, considering that it might not be returned or might be misinterpreted.

Still, there is an interesting dynamic at work when two strangers encounter one another. Often one or the other briefly struggles with the decision of whether or not to dare a smile. It seems a rather pointless dilemma when one considers the possible consequences: He/she may not reciprocate. So what? You did what was natural for you and so did the other person. It doesn't take too much effort since more effort is involved when one frowns. Also, there is a 50–50 chance that your smile will be returned. In this case, two people have become just a little less like strangers, a little less alone.

A smile can say many things in many situations. Without it we would be greatly restricted in our dealing with other people. Anyone who would doubt that might want to try going through a day without a smile. If it turns out to be an easy thing to do, I'd be a little concerned. For most of us, our smiles come naturally and are an expression of being fully alive. William James wrote that we are happy *because* we smile, not the reverse. That's something to think about.

It's interesting that our very first smiles appeared shortly after birth without any prompting from anyone.

Psychologists have learned that the smile is a prerequisite to later positive relationships. Paul Eckman, a California psychologist, once conducted studies among various cultures to determine which facial expressions were universally recognized. In literate and preliterate cultures, the one image that was consistently identified was the portrait of a smiling face.

I'm partial to all kinds of smiles which come directly from the heart and end in a full laugh. I love the kind of smile that comes to a person who is quietly remembering a beautiful moment in the past or anticipating joy to come. And there is the magical smile between two people which is the perfect complement to meeting for the first time. It's the most direct way of saying, without words, "I'm truly glad to know you." And I love that wonderful smile on parents' faces when their child has done something especially well.

If you'll study you own face, you'll discover that the lines which extend from the corners of the nose to the sides of the mouth are the ones formed when we smile. They are the first and usually most pronounced lines that appear on the face. They seem to follow a natural contour. If William James was right about our being happy because we smile, we are all blessed with an abundant source of happiness.

We are in the midst of a communication revolution and the emphasis these days seems to be on speed and efficiency. But I can't help wondering whatever happened to the art of letter writing. We seem to have forgotten how to do it. Words are taped, transcribed and processed these days. Letters are considered passé as long as a phone is handy; we say it saves us time and energy. So we lose yet another personal touch.

On the other hand, businesses and corporations have rediscovered the value of the personal letter in their dealings with the public. Think of all those form letters we receive which try so hard to sound personal. They even call us by our first name. The illusion is almost perfect. We are supposed to believe that someone is some distant marketing firm cares enough to write us a personal note.

I'm sure that the people who send these letters know they're not fooling anyone. But they also understand a little basic human psychology. People are more apt to pay attention to a message that acknowledges them personally. It certainly beats "occupant," "homeowner," or "to whom it may concern."

We are naturally drawn to a letter, especially one which comes to us in a handwritten envelope. They seem so rare. We recognize that a letter takes time and effort, and that's why it's so well received.

The problem is that we think we need to be a Virginia Woolf or Marcel Proust when we communicate something in writing. We worry about poor grammar, bad spelling and all the rules that guided us through school essays and compositions. We think we must be literary or poetic or terribly clever when we say it in writing. We forget that it is sufficient to know that someone cared enough to send a personal message.

I get cards and letters written on the strangest things. They're very often scribbled notes with no literary pretensions, just something to keep in touch, share love or say hello. Not long ago I received a postcard with only three words on it. The salutation: "Leo," the body: "Ugh," and the closing: "Me." The "ugh" was an opinion of a Broadway play I had asked my friend to send along after he had seen it. A lengthy description would not have been nearly as eloquent as that one-word message.

And there's another advantage to letter writing that we don't often think about. It allows us the opportunity to say exactly what we feel. We have time to reflect and put things just the way we want them. I'm all for face-to-face communication, but for whatever reason, we don't always say in person what we really feel. Sometimes it helps to sort out our feelings in quiet, then capture them on paper. Even if no one else appreciates it, it has value in helping to clarify things in our own mind.

Have you ever thought about why we save letters we've received over the years and count them among our private treasures? Why else do we read and reread them, each time letting the words impart their meaning as if for the first time? What else could account for mail carriers' popularity except their bringing such letters to us. Certainly they bring other things too, but I'd venture to say that one personal letter from someone we care about is worth five of any other kind.

My sister Lee has saved all of my letters from my many travels, going back nearly thirty years. I only discovered this a few months ago while sitting around a dinner table savoring one of her great dining experiences. "Remember all those letters you used to write me from Europe and the Orient?" she asked. "Well, here they are." And with that she placed a box full of memories on my lap. The collection was a living narrative of places and people and experiences that up to now were only dimming memories. I was reminded of an old and very wise saying from the Orient: The strongest memory is paler than the weakest ink.

How few modern lovers will know the joy of rereading that bundle of letters, tied with ribbon, preserved over the years as a lasting narrative of a growing love. We have so many ways to communicate with each other. Sometimes it seems as if putting pen to paper is the most neglected one. There's so much we can accomplish with the right words at the right time. Why not put it in writing?

One of the most interesting communication problems I've heard of was between two individuals who had been married for twenty years. After all those years the husband seemed to consciously turn off his wife's statements. He never seemed to hear her. She would ask him to do something, and he would sit there sphinx-like, even when she became noticeably perturbed with him for not answering. I wondered about this behavior. His explanation was fascinating.

"I don't ignore her. My doctor told me that I'm deaf to high frequency tones. When my wife is angry, her voice registers about a half an octave higher. I can't hear her. Of course she doesn't believe a word of it."

Indeed his wife was not easily convinced that when he turned a deaf ear to her (so to speak), his listening problem was physiological. I suspect, along with her, that he took full advantage of his condition to screen out all sorts of unpleasant communications. Happily, their love is strong enough to overcome the problem.

Really listening to others is an art—one that we must be continually cultivating. It is so much more than just hearing words and reacting to them. I believe the very best in us is brought out when we truly listen to others, because to do so requires some of the noblest of human traits. "I listen to you because I respect you. I want to know you. I want to understand you better." "I listen to you because I feel with you, knowing that I will need your compassion one day, too." "I listen to you because I love you."

So many of us are working so hard at making ourselves

heard, that we forget that the better half of communicating is *listening*. We have all experienced the distress of talking to people who are so self-absorbed that they are not hearing a word we say—all the while preparing dazzling responses of their own. Diogenes might have had just such people in mind when he wrote over two thousand years ago, "We have two ears and only one tongue in order that we may hear more and speak less." If you keep talking, you just hear yourself say what you already know.

Then there are those whose attention may be won for only brief periods. As you talk, they will glance in every other direction but your eyeballs, which is where they should look when you are talking to them. Sometimes they will even engage others in the middle of a conversation and you are left talking to yourself. They seem to be suffering from the delusion that their attention is so precious that it can only be given in limited quantities. Whatever, it is one of the worst insults one human being can give to another.

A story of one of my college students illustrates just how critical listening can be. She had been battling a severe depression and was trying to communicate her problems to her parents. More than once she spoke to them of her world caving in around her, and her parents, for whatever reason, chose not to hear. She even went so far as to tell them that she had contemplated suicide, and still her parents did not listen. When she finally did attempt suicide, and fortunately failed, the mother and father were dumbstruck. You can imagine this young woman's frustration when they asked, "Why didn't you tell us you were having problems?"

It is ironic that where good communication is the most critical, it is often in its sorriest state. The people who are the closest to us in life are very often assumed to be the most predictable and therefore are often the least listened to because of it. When we close people out, so much more is neglected than just good conversation. There is the greater harm in being indifferent to the growth and change that constantly takes place in each of us. We must remind one another that every day finds each of us a little changed from the day before. If we fail to listen, we are one day likely to be faced with a stranger. Each day there is a new you waiting to unfold and be discovered by anyone who will take the time to listen.

It was on the day the Russians informed the world that they were boycotting the Los Angeles Olympic Games. That same evening I happened to see an interesting confrontation on television between representatives of the Soviet and American governments. The subject, of course, was the boycott. The atmosphere was quite tense.

First the gentleman from our State Department launched a scathing attack on the Russian government. He brought up every negative thing it had done for the last five years. Not a hint of conciliation in his approach. It was a cardinal opportunity to take the offensive and it was seized with determination.

The rebuttal from the Soviet representative returned in kind what was hurled at him. He dredged up every complaint and example, real or imagined, of American wrongdoing that he could manage in the few minutes allotted him.

It was a standoff. Both men apparently did what habit and tradition dictated under the circumstances. Each had a position to advance or defend and it was done forcefully and without compromise. What made this exchange a memorable one for me was the presence of a third participant in the dialogue. After the partisans had dug their trenches, the president of the U.S. Olympic Committee, Peter Ueberroth, was asked to comment.

At that time, his sole concern was the full participation of *all* countries in the Olympics. He seemed to better understand the need to steer a middle course, so he artfully directed the dialogue toward the question of what could be done to everyone together. It had a much nicer ring than, "Look what you've done wrong lately."

After this there was a noticeable change in the atmosphere. The adversaries seemed to relax their posture a little and even though neither was willing to see things differently, at least the harshness was gone. All it took was a little tact. One would think that diplomats, as we like to call them, would be a little better practiced in this skill.

We'd like to think that the people in whom we place so much faith will understand the power and the effect of their words and use them wisely, for all our sakes. We come to realize, however, that our leaders and our spokespersons are capable of the same miscalculations as the rest of us in our communications with others.

We're daily given the choice of trampling on people's feelings, or being a little considerate. The latter usually requires nothing more than thinking before we speak. It's really not a very demanding proposition, but as we all know, some people have difficulty in this area.

We all like to be straightforward in our dealings with others, but we realize also that honesty sometimes requires a measure of kindness. Still, we have those who are of the opinion that their perception of the world is the stuff honesty is made of. They'll tell you when they don't like the tilt of your hat or the consistency of your noodle casserole. If they disagree with you, they'll always let you know because not to do so, in their view, is to violate the truth. They would never preface a comment with "The way I see it," rather, they explain, "Well, to be perfectly honest . . . "

and follow this with a brutal frankness that nobody could appreciate. As children these individuals were no doubt treasured for their candid nature and natural innocence. But as adults they can be pretty difficult individuals to be around.

Frankness is not necessarily honesty. Happily most of us learn to cultivate a sense of reserve out of simple consideration for others. True honesty includes a measure of goodwill because we recognize that truth may be hurtful or malicious. I don't believe that among lovers and friends there should be no reserve. Even the most loving couple must be careful. Some undeveloped or spontaneous remarks are often better left unspoken. Thoughts verbalized in moments of despair, suspicion, anger or condemnation can often be permanently damaging to a relationship.

Tactfulness, on the other hand, is being careful to pick the best time for all concerned. Even saying nothing may be the sort of tact that is just right for the situation. Of course, that may mean holding back that perfect retort or saving the "I told you so" for another day.

Those who can temper frankness with thoughtfulness are to be admired. We need more of that kind of honesty in our relationships, as well as in the political arena. We all benefit from honest communication, but especially when it is mixed with a little tact.

Once someone is labeled, it's difficult to change the image it creates.

Three years ago *Time* and *Newsweek* did profiles on me. In the headlines I was described as *Dr. Hug* in *Time*, and *The Prince of Hugs* in *Newsweek*. These tags were not meant to be derogatory, just the usual eye-catching media hype. It worked. Since then I have never appeared on television or radio, or been written about in a newspaper article without being associated with the *hug* label.

The sad part of such labeling is that it suggests I am a gimmicky individual who, by hugging everyone in sight, is not to be taken seriously. This is hardly what a person who has dedicated his life to the better understanding of human love would hope for. It's true that I value hugs. In fact, I feel they are essential to good health and a long life. People feel isolated and lonely without them. Hugging is natural and I have never thought of it as any big deal.

I was raised in a large Italian family where a hug and a kiss on both cheeks was expected. In fact, it was a punishable offense not to hug grandma, grandpa and the long stream of friends and relatives who regularly passed through our home.

It didn't take long to discover, however, that not all the world loves a hugger. I was reprimanded by teachers and shunned by many of my peers who thought me weird. It seemed sad and puzzling to me that I had to be cautious of whom I hugged and under what circumstances I hugged them. It also made me unhappy to think that many were missing the joy and contentment a hug produced.

In my travels outside the United States, I became delightfully aware that in most countries people hugged and kissed in greeting. In Asia, for example, men and women alike walk hand in hand, arm in arm.

However, in my media tour of England when my book *Living, Loving & Learning* was published there, hugging caused a minor sensation. The media announced my arrival by saying that "Dr. Hug" from the United States was coming to change Britons' habits. One London newspaper even sent a group of attractive women through the city to hug people at random and make notes for what the paper called a scientific survey. The results were surprising— even to them. Most people interviewed said they loved the human contact and wished there were more of it in their country. There were, however, those who felt it infringed on their space or that it was appalling.

Year after year we are presented with interesting and verifiable research that suggests hugging is healthy. *Touch Therapy*, by Helen Colton, teaches how touching can enhance one's life. To my knowledge no one has claimed that a warm, caring hug can be detrimental to your health. Wherever I speak, people line up and wait for hours to share a friendly hug, often decrying the fact that they get so few and need them so much.

Isn't it interesting how we reserve our embraces for such intense emotional occasions as sexual acts, moments of extreme elation, tragedy or catastrophe? We rush into the security of another's arms after earthquakes, floods, and accidents. Men, who might never do so otherwise, pat and hug each other with wild abandon after winning a game or accomplishing a successful athletic feat. Family members gathered at a funeral find special comfort and tenderness in each other's arms, even though it is not customary for them to be affectionate with one other.

It is natural for us to want to show affection, but for some mysterious reason we equate tenderness with sentimentality, weakness and vulnerability. We are often as hesitant to give a hug as to receive it.

So what's the big deal? Hugging is a very human affirmation of being valued and cherished. It feels good, costs nothing and requires little effort. It's healthy for both the hugged and the hugger.

So have you hugged your wife, husband, father, mother, child, grandmother, grandfather, mother-in-law, father-in-law, neighbor, coworker, priest, minister, psychologist, boss lately?

A
Passion
for
Empathy

Papa used to tell me, "Felice, it costs nothing to be nice," and after waiting for the wisdom of that to settle in my mind, he would always follow with, "And you get so much in return."

"Put yourself in my shoes." It's a familiar request. Perhaps the phrase is derived from the native American Sioux who said never to judge another until you had walked for two weeks in his moccasins. We usually say it because someone doesn't understand what we're feeling and we'd like them to identify with us. It reassures us that we're not alone in facing our problems. In short, we need their empathy.

The dictionary defines empathy as "having the capacity to participate in the ideas and feelings of another." It's a very special human quality that allows us to step outside of ourselves and try to understand another person from within. Often, no words are necessary. Feelings are conveyed even when we don't have the ability to describe them.

From one of Grimm's tales comes a poignant example of just how important empathy (or lack of it) can be. Some of us might remember "Grandfather's Corner," the story of an old man who lived with his son and his son's wife. The father was almost deaf and blind and had difficulty eating without spilling his food. Occasionally he would drop a bowl and break it. The son and his wife thought it was disgusting and made him eat in a corner behind the stove. They gave him a wooden bowl which couldn't be broken.

One day the little grandson was working with some pieces of wood. When this father asked what he was doing, he replied, "I'm making a trough for you and mother to eat out of when I'm grown up." From that moment on, his grandfather rejoined the family at the table and no one ever said another word about it.

The realization that, "I, too, may be there one day," is a splendid teacher of empathy. Surely we can all foresee a time when our needs will be different and we just may require a little extra care and compassion. Of all the human qualities which make us feel connected to each other, I believe it is the ability to empathize that draws us closest.

All of us have known rejection and failure in one form or another. From these experiences we understand just that much better the disappointment or the despair of others. Part of the strength that comes with adversity is the forming of empathy. Not only do we learn to feel with others, but we're also less apt to judge them.

One of the most interesting examples of empathy I've ever heard comes from George Orwell, writing about his experiences during the Spanish Civil War in *Such Were the Days*. It was in the heat of battle when he had his gun trained on a soldier of the other side who, in that instant, was quite literally caught with his pants down. Seeing him in such a vulnerable position Orwell writes that he was unable to pull the trigger. The enemy suddenly appeared all too human.

Perhaps it would be well for us to pause from time to time before speaking or doing something and ask ourselves, "How would I feel if this were said or done to me?" We have been taught to follow the Golden Rule all our lives, not that we may become shining examples of behavior, but that we realize one more way of better understanding one another. So put yourself in my shoes, or anyone else's who needs your understanding and compassion.

When was the last time that you were complimented for anything? I recently spoke to a mother of seven who told me that she hadn't heard the word *thanks* for over five years. Expressed compliments and praise are rare these days.

Not too long ago I was asked to speak to a group of sorority girls. I was overwhelmed with the kindness, the poise and loveliness of those young ladies present. I freely shared my delight. I commented about the wisdom of one girl's statement, the lovely color of another's dress, the brightness of another's smile, and the thoughtfulness of still another. As the evening progressed, one of the girls suggested that I seemed to compliment a bit too freely.

"Don't you?" I asked.

"Why should I?" she was quick to respond. "No one compliments me!"

"I compliment because I feel that it makes me feel good and it makes others happy. Isn't that reason enough?" I asked her. "It's such an easy thing to do."

She wasn't convinced. She was certain that I must be phony or have some ulterior motive.

On the other hand, I have noticed that people are often embarrassed when they are complimented. They become suspicious and get that "What's he after?" look on their faces.

"What a lovely outfit!" I say.

"Oh, this old rag!" they answer, "I've had it for years." It's difficult to understand why anyone would wear an old rag they'd had for years unless they still cared enough about it to be seen in it. An ordinary, "Oh, thank you. I like it too," would seem a healthier response.

But it is understandable that living in a society in which we feel awkward giving compliments would not prepare us for receiving them. Yet, most of us need to be praised from time to time. Compliments are a needed expression of affirmation, of being seen and approved. We emerge from such experiences feeling more complete, more joyful, more confident. After all, there is nothing wrong with desiring approval. It's a natural trait of being human. If we don't desire recognition, why do we spend hours grooming, primping, deodorizing, selecting our clothes and hairdressers so carefully?

It seems to me that we need never fear saying something kind to someone, even a stranger. Perhaps the reception will not always be what we had hoped, but never mind, in the long run, it will be appreciated. We experience so few compliments that when we do get them it is like most unexpected happenings; it puts us off balance. Think about many parents, for example, who are so often ready to criticize but less apt to comment on the good their children do. They forget that constant faultfinding does little but produce hate and avoidance reactions. But when there is an equal amount of praise offered for things well done, then the criticism becomes more tolerable and has a more lasting effect.

Certainly there is something good, something beautiful, something positive in everyone. I recently saw an elderly lady with a beautiful wine-colored, velvet hat perched saucily on her graying hair. She sat buried in a newspaper in the waiting room of a doctor's office. I decided to respond to my instinct and leaned over to her. "You look lovely in that hat. It's a wonderful color." She put down her paper and smiled warmly. "I love hats!" she said. "I'm glad you noticed it." This was the start of a long, animated conversation. She became radiant and even more lovely. Our wait seemed so much shorter. It cost me nothing. It helped us both to feel more joyful. When I left, I wondered how many people there had admired the hat, but had said nothing. It takes so little energy and everyone gains. Try it and experience for yourself the pure magic that is in a word of praise.

Every generation has had its critics of teenagers. In ancient Greece, Socrates lamented their bad manners and contempt for authority. St. Paul, writing about five hundred years later, described the youth of Rome as "filled with wickedness, rottenness, greed and malice." The very word teen comes from an old Anglo-Saxon word (teona) which means vexation.

No doubt many generations have felt slightly vexed by adolescent behavior and attitudes, but there's also that abundance of energy and exciting sense of beginning that are so much a part of this time of life.

Teenagers. What are they up to now? Pink and orange hair, outrageous clothes, bizarre music, a language all their own, a lack of respect for established values—in other words, nothing really out of the ordinary. Not that all teens can be identified with this image, but they do seem to cause a good deal of concern for the present generation of adults.

Recently I visited an old friend whose daughter is in her middle teens. The last time I had seen her she was in pigtails and missing some front teeth. Now she wore a plastic hand grenade as an earring and a bondage belt around her waist. Her clothes were disheveled and the colors clashed horribly (or from her standpoint, perfectly). To complete this ensemble, she wore combat boots.

She had indeed changed from the cute little munchkin I remembered; but after talking to her for a while, she seemed a typical teenager.

Much has been written about this so-called difficult period—gallant attempts to help confused parents better understand what is going on in the teenage mind. We are told that adolescents are going through an identity crisis, a hazy area between childhood and adulthood. It is a time of identity confusion, of peer pressure, of sexual awakening. It is a period to begin developing a philosophy of life, questioning truths and seeking heroes and answers. These can be unsettling things which cause us to throw up our arms to heaven, shake our heads and wonder, as every generation has, just where this is all leading us.

Letters I've received express a sincere concern with, as one woman put it, "young people's preoccupation with the devil." She illustrates her belief with "their song lyrics, their sacrilegious jewelry, and those shocking performances." Though not to such an extreme, I must confess to being a little bewildered by some of these things myself. Up to now, my idea of a wild outfit has been a plaid, multicolored sport coat with yellow pants. Musically speaking, I don't suppose I'll ever understand a group with a name like Johnny Rotten and the Sex Pistols.

But then that's not the sort of understanding teenagers need anyway. I think the very least we can do is try to remember our own adolescence and even if we were models of stability, we can certainly recall what a volatile period it was. Surely it's possible for us to attempt to understand and offer guidance without too much criticism.

Teenagers are people involved in their own kind of struggle. Just like the rest of us, they sometimes need to work them out in their own way, at their own pace. What they need is support and understanding, not put-downs.

No doubt today's teenagers will be the next generation's critics, and it seems to me there's a natural order to it all. They'll know they've made the transition when they begin to preface statements with, "When I was your age. . ." and then proceed to explain a better way. We can easily forget that it's possible for others to benefit from our experience without their having to duplicate it.

Some of the most conservative, proper people today were children of the 60's and 70's. They were called hippies. I remember so well how they stirred up the more settled members of society with their appearance, their music and their philosophy. I would venture a guess that most of yesterday's hippies find themselves in very different roles today, none the worse for the shocking experiences of their youth. Those of us who view the excesses of today's teenagers with a sense of alarm might consider yesterday's "love children," the majority of whom are living with home mortgages and raising sons and daughters through measles and braces.

Personally, I can't think of anything more exciting than young people coming to grips with their own uniqueness as individuals. We all did it, and happily, most of us survived. Adolescence is the natural time for this. We can do no less than help them to do the same.

A
Passion
for
All Stages
of Life

I remember quite clearly an old photo of Papa that was pasted with care in our family album. It was his earliest picture as a young boy and the only likeness of him that survived his childhood. More than anything, I remember those vital and gentle eyes shining through the old and weathered picture. It was a look that he carried throughout his life.

When I feel age encroaching, I remember those eyes and think of the things about Papa that defied time. I am again reminded that what is essential in all of us is ageless. Beginnings and endings are united when we understand that aging may be simply a continuous process from innocent childhood to sophisticated childishness.

It is painfully apparent to anyone who knows me or my work that food happens to be among my greatest passions. For me, it's one of life's immense pleasures. When I was a child, I hated food. It saddens me to think of the wonderful meals Mama and Papa cooked that deserved a great deal of appreciation. I ate only to stay alive. I was a skinny kid, though this may be difficult to believe for anyone seeing me now. Everyone coaxed me and pleaded lest I fade away or die of malnutrition.

Eating became less a problem as I grew into young adulthood, but my weight remained the same. Times and styles change and what was formerly seen as the cure of *thin* had become a blessing. Diet-conscious friends were more than a little envious of me as I ate with abandon without any observable effect. As others struggled with the battle of the bulge, I approached every dining experience with the assurance that it would never happen to me.

"It will in time," I was told by more pudgy friends. "Wait 'til you hit thirty. You'll see." I did.

At about thirty-five, I began to expand. I was appalled to find that the body is actually inflatable. For the first time in my life it became obvious that I needed to exercise some discipline over what I put into my mouth. By this time, of course, I'd formed a passionate love affair with food. Meals had become a special delight rather than just a pause to refuel.

The endless varieties of fish, meat, vegetables all smothered in rich hollandaise, bechamel and assorted cream and butter-based sauces had become an anticipated source of pleasure. Breakfast, lunch and dinner were much-waited-for-rituals, all of which were punctuated with coffee cake, sweet rolls and outlandish desserts. It was like having finally discovered one of life's true miracles only to have it torn abruptly away.

The irony of it all! In the ensuing years people began

to comment that I was looking "especially healthy." I was hearing words such as *paunch* and *pleasingly plump*.

Many can no doubt identify with this depressing happening: the sudden discovery that your trousers or skirts have shrunk and seem more like tourniquets than clothing. We soon become a part of a whole fraternity involved in a similar awakening. We also become even more painfully aware of those not yet affected.

We assure ourselves that the boyish or girlish figure can be regained with just a little sacrifice. We become determined to adopt a healthful regimen of diet and exercise. We begin to jog and/or lift weights. We skip desserts. Chocolate becomes something to dream of but never to consume. Late night snacks are a definite taboo. A new concept of eating gradually sinks in. It's called moderation.

But to our horror, all seems to no avail. Very little seems to affect the expanding bulge. We call on humor to salve our pain. We begin to refer to our excess inches by endearing names, like love handles. We buy clothes a size larger and blame it on the cut of the items. We pass mirrors more swiftly than before.

One of my nephews just turned thirty. He tells me that he's joined a gym, that he'll never lose his lifeguard physique. For his sake I hope he won't, but I have my doubts when I watch him put away food. (How many miles must one run at thirty to work off five calories?)

I guess the only comfort lies in the fact that a spreading mid-section happens to most of us. It becomes, therefore, a common bond and as far as I'm concerned, anything that brings us together can't be all bad!

Years ago, when I was teaching my Love Class at the University of Southern California, I asked my students to write a short history of the lives of their parents. They stared blankly at me. "A history of our parents!" They were incredulous. "What do you mean?"

A short history, I explained, about where they came from, how they met, their special moments of joy or pain. A history.

It became quickly apparent that they knew nothing about their family histories. When challenged, the majority of the students didn't even know the exact color of their parents' eyes. It hadn't occurred to them that Mom and Dad had ever courted and loved! It was impossible for some of them to accept the fact that their mother had ever received a first kiss or had gone on dates that may not have included their father!

This lack of awareness is not confined to my students. Most of us take those we love for granted. We assume that they are there and will always be there when we need them. Not so!

I recall the after-dinner talking time in our home when I was a child. I can't tell you how many times we asked Mama to tell us about her years as a young servant girl to the Padrone. The indignities. The insults. The inhumane treatment. How vivid were her descriptions of the crowded immigrant ship on which she came to America, her long stay on Ellis Island with her sick child, the train trip to Los Angeles—unable to speak English, shy and afraid.

Papa's stories of his work at the factory in Italy, of his first job in America, times of extreme poverty, times of genuine joy were of equal interest. We children sat in rapt attention, full of admiration and wonder that our parents had achieved so much. I learned that things didn't start with me. I was a part of an ongoing history full of pride, survival and love.

We do not exist in isolation, we are a part of a greater story, some of it having been written, some which we will write, and some which we will pass on to others to complete.

At a recent book fair I found a most interesting softcover book. As I recall, it was called something like, *Father Was Quite a Boy*. A companion book was called, *Mother Was Quite a Girl*. These books were simply a series of open-end questions for mama and papa to fill in. Describe your parents. What was the name of your first boyfriend? Who took you to your prom? Etc. When completed, these books were to be given to the children as part of their legacy. What a splendid idea! What a long-lasting and valuable gift.

So often we are too concerned with tomorrow to recognize the significance of yesterday. Yet that represents the thread of explanation which guides us to who we are now.

I can't tell you the joy my students felt when they completed their assignment. For some, it was the best time the family had experienced together in years. "Did you know my dad first worked on a railroad?" "My mother waited tables when she was in high school." "My mother was my father's buddy's girlfriend. Dad won a wife but lost a friend." "Mama had a miscarriage which still brings her sorrow." "Dad married his first wife when she was only seventeen." "I had no idea my mom was such a hellion when she was my age!"

We all agreed that it would have been a tragedy to have missed the experience of the past. "It scares me," one student said, "when I think that my parents could have died and I wouldn't have known them at all!"

We owe each other a knowledge of the past. It's a shared bond from which we gain the knowledge and strength to face our tomorrows!

• • •

Just a few years ago I found myself in a hospital intensive care unit. I awakened in a large, noisy room with a number of other patients lying about in various stages of devastating ailments. There were respirators, intravenous tubes, bottles, catheters, a host of monitoring devices suspended from everywhere. Being there myself was trauma enough—I had no desire to inflict this scene upon friends and relatives. I gave specific instructions that I was to receive no visitors. I was told that I would be out of intensive care, if all went well, within twenty-four hours. Then I would see people.

That room was a lonely place. I know it seems strange that in a place where you are never long out of sight of a trained, watchful eye one can be so lonely, so frightened, so confused and alone. But so it was. I didn't realize how much I needed the people I knew and loved. I needed to see a friendly face—not an efficient one, but a loving one. I needed to feel a warm touch—not a professional touch, but a tender one.

At that point I was awakened by the sound of the door opening quietly behind me. Not the door which led into the cluttered room, but the one that opened to the corridor outside. I thought I might be having a dream, or that perhaps the drugs I'd been given were bringing on a hallucination. But there he was. My very dear friend. He walked cautiously between the respirator, the I.V. tubes and other equipment, smiled down at me and took my hand. It was a moment of sheer magic. I forgot the horror of the room—the tubes, the bottles, the noise. I didn't matter how he had gotten in or whether he would soon be asked to leave. A human being whom I loved was near and sharing my experience. I'll remember this moment forever.

It is ironic that when people need us most we are often least able to give. This is especially true at times of serious illness or impending death. I'm certainly as guilty as everyone else. It happens every time when someone in my family or a dear friend is ill or in a hospital. I am torn between wanting to be near them and a strange feeling of wanting to avoid having to see them. Emotionally I feel this confusion, even though I feel strongly that no one should suffer alone or die alone.

Things were different in generations past. The critically ill were kept in the home and lovingly nursed and attended to. It was a family member who tenderly closed their eyes for the last time. Only death could separate them. Perhaps what has happened is that we have allowed ourselves to be intimidated by medical jargon and hospitals. The result has been understandable feelings of inadequacy and fear. We feel that we have no part in our loved ones' recuperation, that we may indeed be jeopardizing their health by keeping them at home. So we have relinquished our potential roles in the healing process.

It is natural that when people feel ill or are dying they want to be at home. They want to be near those they have loved for so many years and who have loved them in return. They want to be in the home and in the bed where they feel most at ease. Yet the moment they most need this loving support system, they are ambulanced away to isolation or intensive-care wards, often to spend their last hours alone or among strangers. So many of us have lost loved ones without ever being able to say goodbye. It can leave us with lasting feelings of sadness, a painful lack of closure.

We must never forget that the person behind the pale face, the pained countenance, or the emaciated body is still the person we love. We must never forget that the need for affection, touching, reassuring, communication and love is still there—only now, intensified.

We all need each other. Perhaps one day we will become ill or incapacitated and require the warmth and tenderness of others. The only way we can be assured that our needs will be fulfilled is to overcome these unrealistic but very human fears, and try to change the process now.

The phrase, old age, aside from being meaningless, more often than not carries with it a negative connotation. Instead of viewing it as a stage of human development, we often look upon it as a disease, characterized by rocking chairs, stooped and ailing bodies, and people who can no longer fend for themselves. Behind it all is the assumption that our later adulthood is something to be dreaded.

In past years there seems to have been a more definable role for the elderly of our society. In many present cultures apart from our own, older members are accorded great deference and are revered *because* of their age and not in spite of it.

With our fetish for youth and all its charms, we are consumed with the idea that there is a prime of life which exists only within certain fixed limits and that it is a fleeting thing. Then, at the first sign that we have gone beyond those limits, we are cast aside and expected to make room for the new generation.

Small wonder that more and more people with the means to do so are settling into retirement communities where they are accepted. For others less fortunate, there are convalescent (why this misnomer?) homes aplenty, which may provide a quiet place in which to live out one's life, but which will never be a substitute for being among loved ones and feeling needed.

When we see reflected in a furrowed and lined face simply a lifetime that is being used up, and nothing more, we disregard a lifetime of accumulated wisdom. We fail to appreciate the imprint of time and the rich tapestry of experiences that is reflected in it. Think what a magnificent storehouse of memories is contained in a full life—the moments of passion, of contentment, of despair, of joy—things that the most sophisticated computer could never retain in its most complicated program. It's interesting that of all the human faculties, long-term memory often remains intact while recent memory fails with age. There is a natural order suggested by this if we consider the price-less treasures that are preserved in the minds of those who have lived long and have so much to pass along to the rest of us.

Our attitudes toward older people will surely determine the world we will know when we ourselves age. If we continue to think of chronological age as an indication of an individual's productivity and capacity for growth, then we effectively mark our own boundaries. Life becomes a succession of closing doors and we begin to say things like, "I'm too old for that," and "Those were the good old days." We agonize over each new gray hair, each wrinkle, as portents of the end.

One of the most common stereotypes of the elderly is that they are bitter or cranky people who have withdrawn from others and often from life in general. The more likely possibility is that we have withdrawn from them.

It is funny to me when I meet young people who see fifty as old. I recently attended a birthday party for a six year old (remember six?). Some of us older folk were trying to give the birthday boy a concept of birthdays and the aging process. He at one point turned to me and asked rather disarmingly, "How old are you?" I responded, evading the question, "How old do you think I am?" "A hundred?" he answered without a moment's hesitation. I'll know better next time.

It's interesting how our attitudes change as we become older. Each stage of life seems to bring with it new needs, beliefs, attitudes and responses. I especially became aware of this when I passed fifty. It is as dramatic as when we pass from childhood to adolescence, or adolescence to adulthood, but we seem less aware of the growing older part of it. There are, however, compensations.

It takes us at least fifty years to finally learn that our life and happiness are not dependent upon any single situation or person. We learn that we don't have to have everything our way, that we don't need to be loved by everyone, and that the world doesn't end if we are rejected.

What a relief finally to know this. We still remember the pain of those first rejections, the feelings of emptiness that seemed to surround us. But after fifty years of living we learn that life will go on, that rejection is merely a part of life and not the end of it. With the perfect vision of hindsight, we wonder why we didn't learn this sooner.

After fifty it seems easier to be ourselves. We realize at last that it takes too much energy to play the game— the game of being what others think we should be. Our priorities change too. For one thing, we don't mind being a little less social. Not having something to do all day Saturday, especially Saturday night, has long ceased to be the tragedy it once was.

Having two or three nights a week booked in advance seems more like obligation than recreation. After fifty we find ourselves looking for excuses to have more time at home to read, watch a good T.V. program or just do nothing. We've even accepted the fact that doing nothing can be doing something. We can say no to an invitation without spending hours planning excuses.

After fifty, our eating and drinking habits seem to

change radically too. Our idea of a late dinner out is 6:30 P.M. and we begin to look at our watches in order to start home by nine. We switch to decaffeinated coffee and light drinks. We give up salted Margaritas and very dry Martinis. We request soda with a twist of lime instead.

Where once we never thought about our health, we now find our cabinets full of multiple vitamins; we swear by our juicer and stock up on high fiber foods. We become aware of our heart beat (where on earth had it been before now?) and know the exact reading of our systolic and diastolic blood pressure. We become more concerned with our vision, our hearing, our skin care, our digestion and our muscle tone. We get practical hairdos, see our dentist more often and go back to Ivory soap.

Our idea of entertainment changes. We tend toward activities which bring us peace, rather than nonstop excitement. We become more choosy about what books we read and what films, plays or television programs we watch. "Let's go to a movie," becomes far more specific and more often means, "Let's go to the local revival theater and see an old Humphrey Bogart or Bette Davis film." We are less tolerant of imperfection in our entertainment and find ourselves more often leaving at intermission. Double features, of course, are out!

I'm certain that as we become 60, 70, or 80 we'll acquire new needs and values, but so it should be. We can look back with fondness at what once was, but also in gratitude for where it has led us. I like to think that these changes are part of the wisdom which comes with age, rather than being a condition that is part of aging.

One of the assignments I gave my counseling students each year always brought on a good deal of controversy and mixed feelings. I would ask my class what they would do if they found they had only five more days to live. Assuming they would be in good health and could do anything they chose, they had to decide how and with whom they would spend their last moments.

Some would wax quite poetic: "I'd go to my favorite spot in Yosemite with my husband/wife/lover." "I'd share my love of nature and die under the stars in my lover's arms." "I'd take a trip to India and spend my last days studying Asian philosophy." Some said they'd seek out the great adventure, gliding free above the earth, diving in the bluest lagoon, climbing where only few have gone. Some wanted to spend their remaining time in quiet introspection or meditation to make final peace with themselves or with God.

But most answers were simple statements: "I'd want to die among those I love." "I'd go home and tell my family I love them." "I'd try to explain my death to my children." "I'd want us to have a big party and see all my family and friends one last time."

Most had in common a strong desire to do something that would make their lives feel more complete, and all with a sense of urgency that always caused me to ask. "Why must you wait for your last five days for doing these things? Why not now?"

Our discussions would often turn to the subject of death and dying and inevitably they became sessions of questions that have no answers. Many had experienced death in one form or another; most had witnessed thousands of deaths on T.V., but all with a remoteness that left them very curious about this great mystery. Though we were unable to agree upon any answers to our questions, I felt there was value in the fact that we openly discussed a subject that is usually shrouded in mystery and fear.

We have more euphemisms to say that someone has

died than for anything else in the English language. People pass on, expire, slip away, or move into the Great Beyond—a thousand other things besides dying. Our avoidance of the word gives us the feeling that it's something to fear. And so we develop inordinate anxieties even to the point of interfering with our happiness now.

Erich Fromm writes, "The whole of life of the individual is nothing but the process of giving birth to himself; indeed we should be fully born when we die." We can think of death as something that stalks us all our lives or we can see it as a reminder that our time is precious. We can put in time until the end comes, or we can use the time we are given to give birth to our potential which is our human trademark.

We often think of death in terms of the tragic circumstances that surround it. We grieve especially for those who are taken prematurely, less I think from a sense of personal loss than from a life that was incomplete. Indeed the greatest tragedy of any death is to reach the end without ever having really lived at all. Why must it take a lifetime to come to this realization? How sad it is to see people who, fearing that the end is near, try frantically to cram all the living they can in the short time left to them. All the things they've ever wanted to do, all the places they've ever wanted to see, all the words that have been left unsaid, suddenly, or rather finally, it dawns on them how precious is their time and how much more they want to really live it.

Our hearts go out to these individuals who must hurry up and live but it seldom occurs to us that there is a message for us all. Whether we think of death as the gateway to the great beyond or as the grim reaper, it still reminds us to give all that we have to the here and now.

Looking back over her incomplete life, Emily, in Thornton Wilder's *Our Town*, laments, "Good-bye world

. . . Goodbye to clocks ticking . . . and Mama's sunflowers. And food and coffee. And new-ironed dresses and hot baths . . . and sleeping and walking up. Oh, earth, you're too wonderful for anybody to realize you."

A lifetime is just too short for us to spend it accumulating regrets for what we might have done. We need to remind ourselves and especially our children, that death is nothing to fear as long as we understand that each moment has a life unto itself with as much possibility for joy and happiness as we are willing to bring to it.

In our time no one is immune from the possibility of violence. No matter how cautious we are, how law abiding, how aware, violence is a very real possibility in our lives. Recently I felt its pain. One of my dearest friends was murdered in a California parking lot. The killers—I am told there were three—ran off and as of this writing have not been apprehended. No matter. My friend is dead. His family, a gentle wife and four children, are suddenly without a husband and father.

The church service was crowded with friends and co-workers, all stunned, angry and bitter. Of course the talk, all in whispers, was about why this should have happened to such a great person. It doesn't make sense that he should have been in the parking lot at the same time as the killers. Why? Idle questions. Conversation without closure. Who on earth knows why?

The priest, rather young, certainly sincere, eulogized my friend. He talked about his important position as vice president of a large department store chain. He talked about his spirituality, his family, his good work. He pointed out that all the truly important things about him were hidden behind a newspaper headline. He said that we live in a headline-oriented society where we read the captions and seldom think about what is behind them—the human element—the only thing which gives the headline meaning. He challenged us to remember the man who will live through our love.

One of his professional colleagues also spoke of Ed. He told of his creativity, his gentleness, kindness and concern. Through his recounting of actual incidents and memories, he awakened in all of us vital experiences we had shared with Ed. For example, it brought to mind his enthusiasm for a family weekend he was initiating, a whole weekend of being together with his son and daughters and their families for meals, golf, talk and general rejoicing. He wanted to be the sole architect of the weekend. He loved them all very much and wanted to demonstrate this in a tangible way.

I saw a strange thing occur as the service progressed. We all became aware of how the family was facing the ordeal with obvious togetherness and love. Interestingly, the congregation was beginning to do the same. Husbands and wives who had entered the church separated were now closer together in the pew, holding hands, crying together, embracing. Children who had raced in ahead of parents were now being cuddled and held. Families were sitting nearer each other. Tears still flowed but more as a reflection of human strength and survival than of pity.

Strange how death and reflection on violence can bring people together as never before. Perhaps death, rather than being a force for separation, is a force for unity. It reminds us of our shared mortality. It tells us that all is temporary. It assures us the time for life is the moment we are living. It ties us together in a common plight and shows us that there is comfort to be had in shared experience.

I have been told that funerals are for the living. Perhaps my experience in the church substantiates that state-

ment. I know that when we got together afterward with
the family and friends, there was a closeness, a caring, an
expiation of pentup pain and sorrow as is seldom felt anywhere when people assemble. Watching my friend's wife
actually comforting all of us and knowing that her pain
was great was a profound experience. Certainly it was an
ending of one aspect of her life, but one could sense that
she had already experienced other endings, none more
tragic or violent, but nevertheless final.

On my way home from the services I had time to reflect. I wondered how many of those who attended the
funeral had felt the overwhelming, saving quality of love
and community at such a time. I wondered how many
would grow from the experience. I also wondered how
soon we would all go our separate ways and forget.

No matter how well we program ourselves for death
and dying it always seems to fill us with dread and fear.
We are rarely prepared to deal with it. As Woody Allen so
aptly put it, "I'm not afraid to die. I just don't want to be
there when it happens."

This seems to have been a year for partings for me.
Three deaths in just a few months. Three wonderful people, creators of memories and generators of love, are no
longer living.

Death is certainly no stranger in my life. Both my parents died several years ago, my grandparents are dead, my
elder brother and several dear friends are all gone. As I
get older I lose more and more loved ones. A friend of
mine who is getting up in age recently recounted the fact
that she has outlived all of her family and most of her close
friends. She lamented that in her rather frail condition it
was becoming too difficult to make new friends. It was not

death that she dreaded so much as the possibility of ending alone, among strangers.

In the past few years much has been done to bring the subject of death out of its shroud. Knowledgeable and caring individuals such as Elisabeth Kübler-Ross, Raymond Moody, and several others have helped us to face the inevitability of death more boldly. The growth of Hospice has further helped us face death and dying with dignity and to part from each other with strength.

Several years ago I wrote a very short book titled *The Fall of Freddie the Leaf*. The message was intended for all ages, but it was written especially for children, to help them understand death as another story in life rather than an abrupt end. I did this because I found so little in the literature that helped me to see death as a positive life force rather than an experience to be dreaded.

The response of book publishers was very enlightening. It revealed one of our prevailing attitudes at that time regarding death. Usually, I was sent form rejection notices without even a personal note. When one was included it was usually to inform me that I must be some kind of a fiend to shock the minds of the young with thoughts of death—what children aren't exposed to certainly can't harm them. My experience with young people told me a different story. After thirty years of teaching, I can't think of many students who didn't experience some kind of loss through death. Their comfort came mostly in the form of condolences instead of any attempt at a rational explanation. My book was written with that need in mind. It took years before I found a publisher who was willing to take the risk. Since then, happily, books relating to the subject have multiplied.

It seems odd to me that we should spend most of our lives avoiding thoughts of death. We convince ourselves that others die, but we prefer not to think of such a thing happening to our loved ones. We act as if we are immortal. We resist accepting our mortality. Even those who believe that only death will bring eternal peace seem to dread the reality.

I believe that it is only acceptance of our mortality that makes us free to live and appreciate the wonder of life. It is death after all that reminds us that we don't have forever, that if we are going to make our statement, express our love for one another, or truly experience life, it must be done now. Death is no respecter of age, social status or economic level. It comes to us all.

I've learned much from those who have died before me. They've taught me that there is no holding on, that we must let go, that there is nothing wrong with tears of parting or the pain of mourning. But the tears eventually must be dried.

Naturally, any death will leave a void in our lives. After all, there are no two individuals the same. But these spaces will be filled with different people, new experiences and new loves.

The Buddha said that every hello is to be seen as the beginning of a new goodbye, that nothing is permanent. But I like to think that every end can also be a beginning, that every goodbye can also be a new hello.

It is not death that we should fear. Rather it is the possibility of a life unlived that is the real tragedy. Perhaps the closer we come to understanding this, the more easily we will come to accept death, and the more fully we will learn to live here and now.

EPILOGUE

Creating and living our personal paradise is not always easy. In a society that is often suspicious of happy, caring and loving individuals, one runs the risk of being dismissed as ridiculous, naive or, as once happened to me, even irrelevant. But what does that matter? It simply suggests that we will have to develop the courage and strength to stand before the critics and cynics and say, "I don't agree with you. Life IS wonderful, joy IS our birthright, and love IS what it's all about," and continue to live life with a passion.

ABOUT THE AUTHOR

Leo Buscaglia, Ph.D., is a professor of education at the University of Southern California. He is in great demand as a lecturer throughout the United States and in many countries abroad.